1000

Days Effortless and Delicious Air Fryer Recipes That Anyone Can Cook at Home | Fry, Bake, Grill & Roast Most Wanted Family

The Essential

Air Fryer

Cookbook 2023

Tobin Deckow

Table of Contents

Chapter 3   Fast and Easy Everyday Favourites   18

Chapter 4   Snacks and Appetisers   24

Chapter 5 Vegetables and Sides

31

INTRODUCTION

Welcome to the new air fryer cookbook where there is a recipe to make virtually every dish that you can imagine.

The rise in the popularity of air fryers began during the early stages of the Covid pandemic when quarantine restrictions necessitated that people cook at home. Inaccessibility to fried fast food inspired people to look for a solution to satiate their craving. Conventional ovens do not easily create the crispy fried food that consumers wanted, and people did not want to deal with the hassle and massive amounts of oil required by a deep fat fryer not to mention a very messy, clean-up process and the need to dispose of the oil after only a limited number of uses. The air fryer provided the perfect solution and is an easy-to-use method of making fried food.

I was a true air fryer sceptic the first time that I heard about them coming into the market, it was only after my friends bought them that I started to have second thoughts. They raved non-stop about how their devices had changed their lives. After trying a sample of the food that was prepared in an air fryer, I had to agree that the food was fantastic. Since purchasing my air fryer, I use it more often than any other method of cooking as it is so easy and convenient.

When I bought my air fryer, I thought that I would only use it for frying food but once I began to understand the different features and cooking modes that it had, I started to experiment with different recipes.

I became so inspired by the variety of food that can be made using an air fryer that I wanted to share my experience with you by writing a cookbook to show just how easy it is to prepare a wide variety of delicious food from basic ingredients that we use every day. Once you have started using our cookbook, you will abandon conventional cooking methods in favour of creating fast, efficient, and tasty meals that require minimal effort to prepare.

The book is simple to read and easy to use and gives you the skills that you need to become an air fryer expert! The book covers everything you need to know about cooking with your air fryer and easy to follow recipes from ingredients that are readily accessible, resulting in meals that are tantalizingly delicious.

Chapter 1 Air Fryer Basic Guide

The first air fryers were produced in 2010 by the German branch of Philips. To better understand the air fryer, we need know how it works.

An air fryer works by harnessing the air and heat from the internal fan which circulates the heat entirely around the slotted basket and helps the food to cook quickly and evenly. The cooking process requires only tiny amounts of oil as compared to normal deep fryers.

A typical air fryer can have up to six different settings: Fry, Crisp, Roast, Bake, Reheat and Dehydrate and creates different types of food.

You can make anything in an air fryer a long as you have the ingredients. Food can also be prepared from frozen in an air fryer so no more waiting for the food to thaw before you cook it.

An air fryer is quite easy to use, and most people should be able to use it with little training. It is surprising how much you can cook in this convenient little gadget; I was surprised and think that you will also be delighted with the amount of time you save when you use it to prepare you next meal.

Why I like the Air Fryer

Less Fat

The ever-growing trend towards healthier eating is achievable by an using an air fryer. You can still enjoy the fried foods that you love but can prepare them with a miniscule amount of oil, still allowing you to enjoy the foods that you love while helping to lower your intake of saturated fats and keeping your cholesterol levels in check.

More Meal Choices

In addition to creating delicious fried food, air fryers come with different cooking settings such as roast, bake and there are models even have a dehydrate function. The possibilities are endless, and you can practically cook any kind of recipe and food in an air fryer.

Less Energy

Air fryers can consume up to 70% less energy than a conventional oven depending on which model you choose which helps keep the electricity bill in check. In addition to be being energy efficient they are also cleaner and safer to use than a deep fat fryer whilst still producing the same wonderful crispy fried food that you love.

Enough Capacity

Big enough to prepare an entire meal for your family – Air fryers range from to two litres in size up to almost ten litres and come in a variety of models each with different features. In short, there is one that will cater perfectly to your requirements.

Faster Meals

Preparation of meals is simple easy and fast, often a hectic lifestyle often does not allow that much for cooking. After a long day at work, the air fryer is perfect as tasty meals can be prepared in twenty minutes with little attention required on the part of the chef and there is limited supervision required during the preparation process.

Different Types of Air Fryers

Cosori Air Fryer

5.5 L in size Has an LED one touch screen with eleven pre-sets, a timer, and temperature control. It comes with a non-stick square basket that is dishwasher safe. Food can be prepared for 3-5 people and is ready 50% faster than a conventional oven. You can cook food that is till frozen. Corosi uses Thermo IQ Technology to maintain a precise temperature and better hot air circulation ensuring the retention of natural juices.

Ninja Foodi Dual Zone Air Fryer

Available in either 7.6 or 9.5 litre sizes, it has two separate programmable cooking zones where two different dishes can be prepared simultaneously. With six different cooking functions – Air Fry, Max Crisp, Roast, Bake, Reheat and Dehydrate – it is perfect for making a full course meal. It cooks 75% faster than a conventional oven and cooks frozen food. It comes with two crisper plates and two 3.8 litre drawers that are easy to remove and are dishwasher safe.

Philips Air Fryer Essential XL

If you are into gadgets then this smart 6.2 litre fryer is the perfect choice for you as it comes equipped with smart wi-fi that is connected to the NutriU App which allows you to monitor and adjust cooking times and temperatures remotely from your phone or tablet and it can be voice controlled through Alexa. Its uses cooks up 40% faster than a conventional oven. The cooking drawer is dishwasher safe.

Instant Vortex Plus with Clear Cook

This 5.7 Litre has an easy-to-use touch screen and 6 in 1 smart programmes, it even includes a dehydration feature. It uses 80% less energy than a conventional oven. You can see through the clear front and the oven has an interior light enabling you to monitor the cooking food without opening the drawer. There is also a progress bar that displays the cooking progress and includes add food and turn food prompts with perfect results every time. Its OdourErase technology has built in air filters that remove cooking smells.

Tower T17021

This 4.3 litre air fryer has a 60-minute timer and uses Vortx technology creating rapid air circulation which results in crisper textures and uses 50% less energy than a conventional oven. It has a variety of different cooking functions such as fry, roast, or bake offering more meal options. The easy use dial control ensures perfectly cooked food every time.

Once you have purchased your new air fryer, our cookbook with its easy-to-follow recipes will help turn you into a professional air fryer chef!

Air Fryer Cooking Tips

1.Cooking with an air fryer assures success every time you prepare a meal.

2.Always pre-heat the unit for around three minutes and coat the fryer basket with oil by rubbing or spraying it lightly on the bottom grates which will prevent food sticking from sticking to the cooking surface.

3.It is important to add the required quantity of your favourite oil to foods that do not contain natural fats.

4.Never over fill the cooking basket as the food will not cook properly.

5.Adjust the temperature and cooking time to avoid food from drying out.

6.Re-apply more oil midway through the cooking process if required.

7.Either shake or flip the items that are cooking such as French fries and chicken wings every few minutes to ensure that everything is evenly cooked.

Air Fryer FAQs

Are air fryers easy to clean?

The removable parts of an air fryer are easy to wash, either in the dishwasher or in warm soapy water. Always ensure that the unit is cool before you wash it.

Do air fryers produce healthier food than when using traditional frying methods?

Air fryers produce healthier food. Acrylamide is a carcinogen that can occur when starchy food such as potatoes when cooked at high temperatures of around 120°C. Air fryers reduce acrylamide levels by up to 90%.

Is the food cooked in an air fryer as good as food that prepared in a conventional oven?

Yes, the air fryer helps to retain food's nutrients as well as natural juices during the air frying process. Air fryer food is just as good or better than recipes cooked in a deep fryer or conventional oven.

Are air fryers safe to use?

Of course, if the used properly air fryers are clean and safe to use as there is no risk of burns from hot oil that splashes or splatters which can happen when using messy deep fat fryers as well the heightened risk of fire from the hot oil.

Chapter 2 Breakfasts

Southwestern Ham Egg Cups

Prep time: 5 minutes | Cook time: 12 minutes | Serves 2

4 (30 g) slices wafer-thin ham

4 large eggs

2 tablespoons full-fat sour cream

60 ml diced green pepper

2 tablespoons diced red pepper

2 tablespoons diced brown onion

120 ml shredded medium Cheddar cheese

Place one slice of ham on the bottom of four baking cups. In a large bowl, whisk eggs with sour cream. Stir in green pepper, red pepper, and onion. Pour the egg mixture into ham-lined baking cups. Top with Cheddar. Place cups into the air fryer basket. Adjust the temperature to 160°C and bake for 12 minutes or until the tops are browned. Serve warm.

Breakfast Pitta

Prep time: 5 minutes | Cook time: 6 minutes | Serves 2

1 wholemeal pitta

2 teaspoons olive oil

½ shallot, diced

¼ teaspoon garlic, minced

1 large egg

¼ teaspoon dried oregano

¼ teaspoon dried thyme

⅛ teaspoon salt

2 tablespoons shredded Parmesan cheese

Preheat the air fryer to 190°C. Brush the top of the pitta with olive oil, then spread the diced shallot and minced garlic over the pitta. Crack the egg into a small bowl or ramekin, and season it with oregano, thyme, and salt. Place the pitta into the air fryer basket, and gently pour the egg onto the top of the pitta. Sprinkle with cheese over the top. Bake for 6 minutes. Allow to cool for 5 minutes before cutting into pieces for serving.

Jalapeño Popper Egg Cups

Prep time: 10 minutes | Cook time: 10 minutes | Serves 2

4 large eggs

60 ml chopped pickled jalapeños

60 g full-fat cream cheese

120 ml shredded sharp Cheddar cheese

In a medium bowl, beat the eggs, then pour into four silicone muffin cups. In a large microwave-safe bowl, place jalapeños, cream cheese, and Cheddar. Microwave for 30 seconds and stir. Take a spoonful, approximately ¼ of the mixture, and place it in the center of one of the egg cups. Repeat with remaining mixture. Place egg cups into the air fryer basket. Adjust the temperature to 160°C and bake for 10 minutes. Serve warm.

Bacon, Egg, and Cheese Roll Ups

Prep time: 15 minutes | Cook time: 15 minutes | Serves 4

2 tablespoons unsalted butter

60 ml chopped onion

½ medium green pepper, seeded and chopped

6 large eggs

12 slices bacon

235 ml shredded sharp Cheddar cheese

120 ml mild salsa, for dipping

In a medium skillet over medium heat, melt butter. Add onion and pepper to the skillet and sauté until fragrant and onions are translucent, about 3 minutes. Whisk eggs in a small bowl and pour into skillet. Scramble eggs with onions and peppers until fluffy and fully cooked, about 5 minutes. Remove from heat and set aside. On work surface, place three slices of bacon side by side, overlapping about ¼ inch. Place 60 ml scrambled eggs in a heap on the side closest to you and sprinkle 60 ml cheese on top of the eggs. Tightly roll the bacon around the eggs and secure the seam with a toothpick if necessary. Place each roll into the air fryer basket. Adjust the temperature to 175°C and air fry for 15 minutes. Rotate the rolls halfway through the cooking time. Bacon will be brown and crispy when completely cooked. Serve immediately with salsa for dipping.

Canadian Bacon Muffin Sandwiches

Prep time: 5 minutes | Cook time: 8 minutes | Serves 4

4 English muffins, split

8 slices back bacon

4 slices cheese

Cooking spray

Preheat the air fryer to 190°C. Make the sandwiches: Top each of 4 muffin halves with 2 slices of bacon, 1 slice of cheese, and finish with the remaining muffin half. Put the sandwiches in the air fryer basket and spritz the tops with cooking spray. Bake for 4 minutes. Flip the sandwiches and bake for another 4 minutes. Divide the sandwiches among four plates and serve warm.

Sausage Stuffed Peppers

Prep time: 15 minutes | Cook time: 15 minutes | Serves 4

230 g spicy pork sausage meat, removed from casings
4 large eggs
110 g full-fat cream cheese, softened
60 ml tinned diced tomatoes,

drained
4 green peppers
8 tablespoons shredded chilli cheese
120 ml full-fat sour cream

In a medium skillet over medium heat, crumble and brown the sausage meat until no pink remains. Remove sausage and drain the fat from the pan. Crack eggs into the pan, scramble, and cook until no longer runny. Place cooked sausage in a large bowl and fold in cream cheese. Mix in diced tomatoes. Gently fold in eggs. Cut a 4-inch to 5-inch slit in the top of each pepper, removing the seeds and white membrane with a small knife. Separate the filling into four servings and spoon carefully into each pepper. Top each with 2 tablespoons cheese. Place each pepper into the air fryer basket. Adjust the temperature to 175°C and set the timer for 15 minutes. Peppers will be soft and cheese will be browned when ready. Serve immediately with sour cream on top.

Egg and Bacon Muffins

Prep time: 5 minutes | Cook time: 15 minutes | Serves 1

2 eggs
Salt and ground black pepper, to taste
1 tablespoon green pesto

85 g shredded Cheddar cheese
140 g cooked bacon
1 spring onion, chopped

Preheat the air fryer to 175°C. Line a cupcake tin with parchment paper. Beat the eggs with pepper, salt, and pesto in a bowl. Mix in the cheese. Pour the eggs into the cupcake tin and top with the bacon and spring onion. Bake in the preheated air fryer for 15 minutes, or until the egg is set. Serve immediately.

Cheddar Eggs

Prep time: 5 minutes | Cook time: 15 minutes | Serves 2

4 large eggs
2 tablespoons unsalted butter, melted

120 ml shredded sharp Cheddar cheese

Crack eggs into a round baking dish and whisk. Place dish into the air fryer basket. Adjust the temperature to 200°C and set the timer for 10 minutes. After 5 minutes, stir the eggs and add the butter and cheese. Let cook 3 more minutes and stir again. Allow eggs to finish cooking an additional 2 minutes or remove if they are to your desired liking. Use a fork to fluff. Serve warm.

Denver Omelette

Prep time: 5 minutes | Cook time: 8 minutes | Serves 1

2 large eggs
60 ml unsweetened, unflavoured almond milk
¼ teaspoon fine sea salt
⅛ teaspoon ground black pepper
60 ml diced ham (omit for vegetarian)
60 ml diced green and red

peppers
2 tablespoons diced spring onions, plus more for garnish
60 ml shredded Cheddar cheese (about 30 g) (omit for dairy-free)
Quartered cherry tomatoes, for serving (optional)

Preheat the air fryer to 175°C. Grease a cake pan and set aside. In a small bowl, use a fork to whisk together the eggs, almond milk, salt, and pepper. Add the ham, peppers, and spring onions. Pour the mixture into the greased pan. Add the cheese on top (if using). Place the pan in the basket of the air fryer. Bake for 8 minutes, or until the eggs are cooked to your liking. Loosen the omelette from the sides of the pan with a spatula and place it on a serving plate. Garnish with spring onions and serve with cherry tomatoes, if desired. Best served fresh.

Pork Sausage Eggs with Mustard Sauce

Prep time: 20 minutes | Cook time: 12 minutes | Serves 8

450 g pork sausage meat
8 soft-boiled or hard-boiled eggs, peeled
1 large egg
2 tablespoons milk
235 ml crushed pork scratchings

Smoky Mustard Sauce:
60 ml mayonnaise
2 tablespoons sour cream
1 tablespoon Dijon mustard
1 teaspoon chipotle hot sauce

Preheat the air fryer to 200°C. Divide the sausage into 8 portions. Take each portion of sausage, pat it down into a patty, and place 1 egg in the middle, gently wrapping the sausage around the egg until the egg is completely covered. (Wet your hands slightly if you find the sausage to be too sticky.) Repeat with the remaining eggs and sausage. In a small shallow bowl, whisk the egg and milk until frothy. In another shallow bowl, place the crushed pork scratchings. Working one at a time, dip a sausage-wrapped egg into the beaten egg and then into the pork scratchings, gently rolling to coat evenly. Repeat with the remaining sausage-wrapped eggs. Arrange the eggs in a single layer in the air fryer basket, and lightly spray with olive oil. Air fry for 10 to 12 minutes, pausing halfway through the baking time to turn the eggs, until the eggs are hot and the sausage is cooked through. To make the sauce: In a small bowl, combine the mayonnaise, sour cream, Dijon, and hot sauce. Whisk until thoroughly combined. Serve with the Scotch eggs.

Gyro Breakfast Patties with Tzatziki

Prep time: 10 minutes | Cook time: 20 minutes per batch | Makes 16

patties
Patties:
900 g lamb or beef mince
120 ml diced red onions
60 ml sliced black olives
2 tablespoons tomato sauce
1 teaspoon dried oregano leaves
2 cloves garlic, minced
1 teaspoon fine sea salt
Tzatziki:
235 ml full-fat sour cream
1 small cucumber, chopped

½ teaspoon fine sea salt
½ teaspoon garlic powder, or 1 clove garlic, minced
¼ teaspoon dried dill, or 1 teaspoon finely chopped fresh dill
For Garnish/Serving:
120 ml crumbled feta cheese (about 60 g)
Diced red onions
Sliced black olives
Sliced cucumbers

Preheat the air fryer to 175ºC. Place the lamb, onions, olives, tomato sauce, oregano, garlic, and salt in a large bowl. Mix well to combine the ingredients. Using your hands, form the mixture into sixteen 3-inch patties. Place about 5 of the patties in the air fryer and air fry for 20 minutes, flipping halfway through. Remove the patties and place them on a serving platter. Repeat with the remaining patties. While the patties cook, make the tzatziki: Place all the ingredients in a small bowl and stir well. Cover and store in the fridge until ready to serve. Garnish with ground black pepper before serving. Serve the patties with a dollop of tzatziki, a sprinkle of crumbled feta cheese, diced red onions, sliced black olives, and sliced cucumbers. Store leftovers in an airtight container in the refrigerator for up to 5 days or in the freezer for up to a month. Reheat the patties in a preheated 200ºC air fryer for a few minutes, until warmed through.

Asparagus and Bell Pepper Strata

Prep time: 10 minutes | Cook time: 14 to 20 minutes | Serves 4

8 large asparagus spears, trimmed and cut into 2-inch pieces
80 ml shredded carrot
120 ml chopped red pepper
2 slices wholemeal bread, cut

into ½-inch cubes
3 egg whites
1 egg
3 tablespoons 1% milk
½ teaspoon dried thyme

In a baking pan, combine the asparagus, carrot, red bell pepper, and 1 tablespoon of water. Bake in the air fryer at 165ºC for 3 to 5 minutes, or until crisp-tender. Drain well. Add the bread cubes to the vegetables and gently toss. In a medium bowl, whisk the egg whites, egg, milk, and thyme until frothy. Pour the egg mixture into the pan. Bake for 11 to 15 minutes, or until the strata is slightly puffy and set and the top starts to brown. Serve.

Maple Granola

Prep time: 5 minutes | Cook time: 40 minutes | Makes 475 ml

235 ml rolled oats
3 tablespoons pure maple syrup
1 tablespoon sugar
1 tablespoon neutral-flavored oil, such as refined coconut or

sunflower
¼ teaspoon sea salt
¼ teaspoon ground cinnamon
¼ teaspoon vanilla extract

Insert the crisper plate into the basket and the basket into the unit. Preheat the unit by selecting BAKE, setting the temperature to 120ºC, and setting the time to 3 minutes. Select START/STOP to begin. In a medium bowl, stir together the oats, maple syrup, sugar, oil, salt, cinnamon, and vanilla until thoroughly combined. Transfer the granola to a 6-by-2-inch round baking pan. Once the unit is preheated, place the pan into the basket. Select BAKE, set the temperature to 120ºC and set the time to 40 minutes. Select START/STOP to begin. After 10 minutes, stir the granola well. Resume cooking, stirring the granola every 10 minutes, for a total of 40 minutes, or until the granola is lightly browned and mostly dry. When the cooking is complete, place the granola on a plate to cool. It will become crisp as it cools. Store the completely cooled granola in an airtight container in a cool, dry place for 1 to 2 weeks.

Breakfast Calzone

Prep time: 15 minutes | Cook time: 15 minutes | Serves 4

350 ml shredded Mozzarella cheese
120 ml blanched finely ground almond flour
30 g full-fat cream cheese
1 large whole egg

4 large eggs, scrambled
230 g cooked sausage meat, removed from casings and crumbled
8 tablespoons shredded mild Cheddar cheese

In a large microwave-safe bowl, add Mozzarella, almond flour, and cream cheese. Microwave for 1 minute. Stir until the mixture is smooth and forms a ball. Add the egg and stir until dough forms. Place dough between two sheets of parchment and roll out to ¼-inch thickness. Cut the dough into four rectangles. Mix scrambled eggs and cooked sausage together in a large bowl. Divide the mixture evenly among each piece of dough, placing it on the lower half of the rectangle. Sprinkle each with 2 tablespoons Cheddar. Fold over the rectangle to cover the egg and meat mixture. Pinch, roll, or use a wet fork to close the edges completely. Cut a piece of parchment to fit your air fryer basket and place the calzones onto the parchment. Place parchment into the air fryer basket. Adjust the temperature to 190ºC and air fry for 15 minutes. Flip the calzones halfway through the cooking time. When done, calzones should be golden in color. Serve immediately.

Easy Sausage Pizza

Prep time: 10 minutes | Cook time: 6 minutes | Serves 4

2 tablespoons ketchup	230 g Mozzarella cheese
1 pitta bread	1 teaspoon garlic powder
80 ml sausage meat	1 tablespoon olive oil

Preheat the air fryer to 170°C. Spread the ketchup over the pitta bread. Top with the sausage meat and cheese. Sprinkle with the garlic powder and olive oil. Put the pizza in the air fryer basket and bake for 6 minutes. Serve warm.

Honey-Apricot Granola with Greek Yoghurt

Prep time: 10 minutes | Cook time: 30 minutes | Serves 6

235 ml rolled oats	1 teaspoon ground cinnamon
60 ml dried apricots, diced	¼ teaspoon ground nutmeg
60 ml almond slivers	¼ teaspoon salt
60 ml walnuts, chopped	2 tablespoons sugar-free dark
60 ml pumpkin seeds	chocolate chips (optional)
60 to 80 ml honey, plus more	700 ml fat-free plain Greek
for drizzling	yoghurt
1 tablespoon olive oil	

Preheat the air fryer to 130°C. Line the air fryer basket with parchment paper. In a large bowl, combine the oats, apricots, almonds, walnuts, pumpkin seeds, honey, olive oil, cinnamon, nutmeg, and salt, mixing so that the honey, oil, and spices are well distributed. Pour the mixture onto the parchment paper and spread it into an even layer. Bake for 10 minutes, then shake or stir and spread back out into an even layer. Continue baking for 10 minutes more, then repeat the process of shaking or stirring the mixture. Bake for an additional 10 minutes before removing from the air fryer. Allow the granola to cool completely before stirring in the chocolate chips (if using) and pouring into an airtight container for storage. For each serving, top 120 ml Greek yoghurt with 80 ml granola and a drizzle of honey, if needed.

Buffalo Chicken Breakfast Muffins

Prep time: 7 minutes | Cook time: 13 to 16 minutes | Serves 10

170 g shredded cooked chicken	1 teaspoon minced garlic
85 g blue cheese, crumbled	6 large eggs
2 tablespoons unsalted butter, melted	Sea salt and freshly ground black pepper, to taste
80 ml Buffalo hot sauce, such as Frank's RedHot	Avocado oil spray

In a large bowl, stir together the chicken, blue cheese, melted butter, hot sauce, and garlic. In a medium bowl or large liquid measuring cup, beat the eggs. Season with salt and pepper. Spray 10 silicone muffin cups with oil. Divide the chicken mixture among the cups, and pour the egg mixture over top. Place the cups in the air fryer and set to 150°C. Bake for 13 to 16 minutes, until the muffins are set and cooked through. (Depending on the size of your air fryer, you may need to cook the muffins in batches.)

Savory Sweet Potato Hash

Prep time: 15 minutes | Cook time: 18 minutes | Serves 6

2 medium sweet potatoes, peeled and cut into 1-inch cubes	1 garlic clove, minced
½ green pepper, diced	½ teaspoon salt
½ red onion, diced	½ teaspoon black pepper
110 g baby mushrooms, diced	½ tablespoon chopped fresh
2 tablespoons olive oil	rosemary

Preheat the air fryer to 190°C. In a large bowl, toss all ingredients together until the vegetables are well coated and seasonings distributed. Pour the vegetables into the air fryer basket, making sure they are in a single even layer. (If using a smaller air fryer, you may need to do this in two batches.) Roast for 9 minutes, then toss or flip the vegetables. Roast for 9 minutes more. Transfer to a serving bowl or individual plates and enjoy.

Spinach and Mushroom Mini Quiche

Prep time: 10 minutes | Cook time: 15 minutes | Serves 4

1 teaspoon olive oil, plus more for spraying	120 ml shredded Cheddar cheese
235 ml coarsely chopped mushrooms	120 ml shredded Mozzarella cheese
235 ml fresh baby spinach, shredded	¼ teaspoon salt
4 eggs, beaten	¼ teaspoon black pepper

Spray 4 silicone baking cups with olive oil and set aside. In a medium sauté pan over medium heat, warm 1 teaspoon of olive oil. Add the mushrooms and sauté until soft, 3 to 4 minutes. Add the spinach and cook until wilted, 1 to 2 minutes. Set aside. In a medium bowl, whisk together the eggs, Cheddar cheese, Mozzarella cheese, salt, and pepper. Gently fold the mushrooms and spinach into the egg mixture. Pour ¼ of the mixture into each silicone baking cup. Place the baking cups into the air fryer basket and air fry at 175°C for 5 minutes. Stir the mixture in each ramekin slightly and air fry until the egg has set, an additional 3 to 5 minutes.

Cheesy Scrambled Eggs

Prep time: 2 minutes | Cook time: 9 minutes | Serves 2

1 teaspoon unsalted butter	cheese
2 large eggs	Salt and freshly ground black
2 tablespoons milk	pepper, to taste
2 tablespoons shredded Cheddar	

Preheat the air fryer to 150°C. Place the butter in a baking pan and cook for 1 to 2 minutes, until melted. In a small bowl, whisk together the eggs, milk, and cheese. Season with salt and black pepper. Transfer the mixture to the pan. Cook for 3 minutes. Stir the eggs and push them toward the center of the pan. Cook for another 2 minutes, then stir again. Cook for another 2 minutes, until the eggs are just cooked. Serve warm.

Pancake Cake

Prep time: 10 minutes | Cook time: 7 minutes | Serves 4

120 ml blanched finely ground almond flour	softened
60 ml powdered erythritol	1 large egg
½ teaspoon baking powder	½ teaspoon unflavoured gelatin
2 tablespoons unsalted butter,	½ teaspoon vanilla extract
	½ teaspoon ground cinnamon

In a large bowl, mix almond flour, erythritol, and baking powder. Add butter, egg, gelatin, vanilla, and cinnamon. Pour into a round baking pan. Place pan into the air fryer basket. Adjust the temperature to 150°C and set the timer for 7 minutes. When the cake is completely cooked, a toothpick will come out clean. Cut cake into four and serve.

Green Eggs and Ham

Prep time: 5 minutes | Cook time: 10 minutes | Serves 2

1 large Hass avocado, halved and pitted	½ teaspoon fine sea salt
2 thin slices ham	¼ teaspoon ground black pepper
2 large eggs	60 ml shredded Cheddar cheese
2 tablespoons chopped spring onions, plus more for garnish	(omit for dairy-free)

Preheat the air fryer to 200°C. Place a slice of ham into the cavity of each avocado half. Crack an egg on top of the ham, then sprinkle on the green onions, salt, and pepper. Place the avocado halves in the air fryer cut side up and air fry for 10 minutes, or until the egg is cooked to your desired doneness. Top with the cheese (if using) and air fry for 30 seconds more, or until the cheese is melted. Garnish with chopped green onions. Best served fresh. Store extras in an airtight container in the fridge for up to 4 days. Reheat in a preheated 175°C air fryer for a few minutes, until warmed through.

Ham and Cheese Crescents

Prep time: 5 minutes | Cook time: 7 minutes | Makes 8 rolls

Oil, for spraying	8 cheese slices
1 (230 g) can ready-to-bake croissants	2 tablespoons unsalted butter, melted
4 slices wafer-thin ham	

Line the air fryer basket with parchment and spray lightly with oil. Separate the dough into 8 pieces. Tear the ham slices in half and place 1 piece on each piece of dough. Top each with 1 slice of cheese. Roll up each piece of dough, starting on the wider side. Place the rolls in the prepared basket. Brush with the melted butter. Air fry at 160°C for 6 to 7 minutes, or until puffed and golden brown and the cheese is melted.

French Toast Sticks

Prep time: 10 minutes | Cook time: 9 minutes | Serves 4

Oil, for spraying	1 teaspoon ground cinnamon
6 large eggs	8 slices bread, cut into thirds
315 ml milk	Syrup of choice, for serving
2 teaspoons vanilla extract	

Preheat the air fryer to 190°C. Line the air fryer basket with parchment and spray lightly with oil. In a shallow bowl, whisk the eggs, milk, vanilla, and cinnamon. Dunk one piece of bread in the egg mixture, making sure to coat both sides. Work quickly so the bread doesn't get soggy. Immediately transfer the bread to the prepared basket. Repeat with the remaining bread, making sure the pieces don't touch each other. You may need to work in batches, depending on the size of your air fryer. Air fry for 5 minutes, flip, and cook for another 3 to 4 minutes, until browned and crispy. Serve immediately with your favorite syrup.

Buffalo Egg Cups

Prep time: 10 minutes | Cook time: 15 minutes | Serves 2

4 large eggs	120 ml shredded sharp Cheddar cheese
60 g full-fat cream cheese	
2 tablespoons buffalo sauce	

Crack eggs into two ramekins. In a small microwave-safe bowl, mix cream cheese, buffalo sauce, and Cheddar. Microwave for 20 seconds and then stir. Place a spoonful into each ramekin on top of the eggs. Place ramekins into the air fryer basket. Adjust the temperature to 160°C and bake for 15 minutes. Serve warm.

Turkey Breakfast Sausage Patties

Prep time: 5 minutes | Cook time: 10 minutes | Serves 4

1 tablespoon chopped fresh thyme	½ teaspoon onion granules
1 tablespoon chopped fresh sage	½ teaspoon garlic powder
1¼ teaspoons coarse or flaky salt	⅛ teaspoon crushed red pepper flakes
1 teaspoon chopped fennel seeds	⅛ teaspoon freshly ground black pepper
¾ teaspoon smoked paprika	450 g lean turkey mince
	120 ml finely minced sweet apple (peeled)

Thoroughly combine the thyme, sage, salt, fennel seeds, paprika, onion granules, garlic powder, red pepper flakes, and black pepper in a medium bowl. Add the turkey mince and apple and stir until well incorporated. Divide the mixture into 8 equal portions and shape into patties with your hands, each about ¼ inch thick and 3 inches in diameter. Preheat the air fryer to 200°C. Place the patties in the air fryer basket in a single layer. You may need to work in batches to avoid overcrowding. Air fry for 5 minutes. Flip the patties and air fry for 5 minutes, or until the patties are nicely browned and cooked through. Remove from the basket to a plate and repeat with the remaining patties. Serve warm.

Apple Rolls

Prep time: 20 minutes | Cook time: 20 to 24 minutes | Makes 12 rolls

Apple Rolls:	sugar
475 ml plain flour, plus more for dusting	1 teaspoon ground cinnamon
2 tablespoons granulated sugar	1 large Granny Smith apple, peeled and diced
1 teaspoon salt	1 to 2 tablespoons oil
3 tablespoons butter, at room temperature	Icing:
180 ml milk, whole or semi-skimmed	120 ml icing sugar
120 ml packed light brown	½ teaspoon vanilla extract
	2 to 3 tablespoons milk, whole or semi-skimmed

Make the Apple Rolls In a large bowl, whisk the flour, granulated sugar, and salt until blended. Stir in the butter and milk briefly until a sticky dough forms. In a small bowl, stir together the brown sugar, cinnamon, and apple. Place a piece of parchment paper on a work surface and dust it with flour. Roll the dough on the prepared surface to ¼ inch thickness. Spread the apple mixture over the dough. Roll up the dough jelly roll-style, pinching the ends to seal. Cut the dough into 12 rolls. Preheat the air fryer to 160°C. Line the air fryer basket with parchment paper and spritz it with oil. Place 6 rolls on the prepared parchment. Bake for 5 minutes. Flip the rolls and bake for 5 to 7 minutes more until lightly browned. Repeat with the remaining rolls. Make the Icing In a medium bowl, whisk the icing sugar, vanilla, and milk until blended. Drizzle over the warm rolls.

Peppered Maple Bacon Knots

Prep time: 5 minutes | Cook time: 7 to 8 minutes | Serves 6

450 g maple smoked/cured bacon rashers	60 ml brown sugar
60 ml maple syrup	Coarsely cracked black peppercorns, to taste

Preheat the air fryer to 200°C. On a clean work surface, tie each bacon strip in a loose knot. Stir together the maple syrup and brown sugar in a bowl. Generously brush this mixture over the bacon knots. Working in batches, arrange the bacon knots in the air fryer basket. Sprinkle with the coarsely cracked black peppercorns. Air fry for 5 minutes. Flip the bacon knots and continue cooking for 2 to 3 minutes more, or until the bacon is crisp. Remove from the basket to a paper towel-lined plate. Repeat with the remaining bacon knots. Let the bacon knots cool for a few minutes and serve warm.

Egg Tarts

Prep time: 10 minutes | Cook time: 17 to 20 minutes | Makes 2 tarts

⅓ sheet frozen puff pastry, thawed	2 eggs
Cooking oil spray	¼ teaspoon salt, divided
120 ml shredded Cheddar cheese	1 teaspoon minced fresh parsley (optional)

Insert the crisper plate into the basket and the basket into the unit. Preheat the unit by selecting BAKE, setting the temperature to 200°C, and setting the time to 3 minutes. Select START/STOP to begin. Lay the puff pastry sheet on a piece of parchment paper and cut it in half. Once the unit is preheated, spray the crisper plate with cooking oil. Transfer the 2 squares of pastry to the basket, keeping them on the parchment paper. Select BAKE, set the temperature to 200°C, and set the time to 20 minutes. Select START/STOP to begin. After 10 minutes, use a metal spoon to press down the center of each pastry square to make a well. Divide the cheese equally between the baked pastries. Carefully crack an egg on top of the cheese, and sprinkle each with the salt. Resume cooking for 7 to 10 minutes. When the cooking is complete, the eggs will be cooked through. Sprinkle each with parsley (if using) and serve.

Baked Potato Breakfast Boats

Prep time: 10 minutes | Cook time: 20 minutes | Serves 4

2 large white potatoes, scrubbed	2 tablespoons chopped, cooked
Olive oil	bacon
Salt and freshly ground black	235 ml shredded Cheddar
pepper, to taste	cheese
4 eggs	

Poke holes in the potatoes with a fork and microwave on full power for 5 minutes. Turn potatoes over and cook an additional 3 to 5 minutes, or until the potatoes are fork-tender. Cut the potatoes in half lengthwise and use a spoon to scoop out the inside of the potato. Be careful to leave a layer of potato so that it makes a sturdy "boat." Preheat the air fryer to 175°C. Lightly spray the air fryer basket with olive oil. Spray the skin side of the potatoes with oil and sprinkle with salt and pepper to taste. Place the potato skins in the air fryer basket, skin-side down. Crack one egg into each potato skin. Sprinkle ½ tablespoon of bacon pieces and 60 ml shredded cheese on top of each egg. Sprinkle with salt and pepper to taste. Air fry until the yolk is slightly runny, 5 to 6 minutes, or until the yolk is fully cooked, 7 to 10 minutes.

Oat and Chia Porridge

Prep time: 10 minutes | Cook time: 5 minutes | Serves 4

2 tablespoons peanut butter	1 L milk
4 tablespoons honey	475 ml oats
1 tablespoon butter, melted	235 ml chia seeds

Preheat the air fryer to 200°C. Put the peanut butter, honey, butter, and milk in a bowl and stir to mix. Add the oats and chia seeds and stir. Transfer the mixture to a bowl and bake in the air fryer for 5 minutes. Give another stir before serving.

Meritage Eggs

Prep time: 5 minutes | Cook time: 8 minutes | Serves 2

2 teaspoons unsalted butter (or	2 tablespoons double cream
coconut oil for dairy-free), for	(or unsweetened, unflavoured
greasing the ramekins	almond milk for dairy-free)
4 large eggs	3 tablespoons finely grated
2 teaspoons chopped fresh	Parmesan cheese (or chive
thyme	cream cheese style spread,
½ teaspoon fine sea salt	softened, for dairy-free)
¼ teaspoon ground black	Fresh thyme leaves, for garnish
pepper	(optional)

Preheat the air fryer to 200°C. Grease two (110 g) ramekins with the butter. Crack 2 eggs into each ramekin and divide the thyme, salt, and pepper between the ramekins. Pour 1 tablespoon of the heavy cream into each ramekin. Sprinkle each ramekin with 1½ tablespoons of the Parmesan cheese. Place the ramekins in the air fryer and bake for 8 minutes for soft-cooked yolks (longer if you desire a harder yolk). Garnish with a sprinkle of ground black pepper and thyme leaves, if desired. Best served fresh.

Mozzarella Bacon Calzones

Prep time: 15 minutes | Cook time: 12 minutes | Serves 4

2 large eggs	60 g cream cheese, softened
235 ml blanched finely ground	and broken into small pieces
almond flour	4 slices cooked bacon,
475 ml shredded Mozzarella	crumbled
cheese	

Beat eggs in a small bowl. Pour into a medium nonstick skillet over medium heat and scramble. Set aside. In a large microwave-safe bowl, mix flour and Mozzarella. Add cream cheese to the bowl. Place bowl in microwave and cook 45 seconds on high to melt cheese, then stir with a fork until a soft dough ball forms. Cut a piece of parchment to fit air fryer basket. Separate dough into two sections and press each out into an 8-inch round. On half of each dough round, place half of the scrambled eggs and crumbled bacon. Fold the other side of the dough over and press to seal the edges. Place calzones on ungreased parchment and into air fryer basket. Adjust the temperature to 175°C and set the timer for 12 minutes, turning calzones halfway through cooking. Crust will be golden and firm when done. Let calzones cool on a cooking rack 5 minutes before serving.

Bacon Cheese Egg with Avocado

Prep time: 15 minutes | Cook time: 20 minutes | Serves 4

6 large eggs	8 tablespoons full-fat sour
60 ml double cream	cream
350 ml chopped cauliflower	2 spring onions, sliced on the
235 ml shredded medium	bias
Cheddar cheese	12 slices bacon, cooked and
1 medium avocado, peeled and	crumbled
pitted	

In a medium bowl, whisk eggs and cream together. Pour into a round baking dish. Add cauliflower and mix, then top with Cheddar. Place dish into the air fryer basket. Adjust the temperature to 160°C and set the timer for 20 minutes. When completely cooked, eggs will be firm and cheese will be browned. Slice into four pieces. Slice avocado and divide evenly among pieces. Top each piece with 2 tablespoons sour cream, sliced spring onions, and crumbled bacon.

Greek Bagels

Prep time: 10 minutes | Cook time: 10 minutes | Makes 2 bagels

120 ml self-raising flour, plus more for dusting

120 ml plain Greek yoghurt

1 egg

1 tablespoon water

4 teaspoons sesame seeds or za'atar

Cooking oil spray

1 tablespoon butter, melted

In a large bowl, using a wooden spoon, stir together the flour and yoghurt until a tacky dough forms. Transfer the dough to a lightly floured work surface and roll the dough into a ball. Cut the dough into 2 pieces and roll each piece into a log. Form each log into a bagel shape, pinching the ends together. In a small bowl, whisk the egg and water. Brush the egg wash on the bagels. Sprinkle 2 teaspoons of the toppings on each bagel and gently press it into the dough. Insert the crisper plate into the basket and the basket into the unit. Preheat the unit by selecting BAKE, setting the temperature to 165°C, and setting the time to 3 minutes. Select START/STOP to begin. Once the unit is preheated, spray the crisper plate with cooking spray. Drizzle the bagels with the butter and place them into the basket. Select BAKE, set the temperature to 165°C, and set the time to 10 minutes. Select START/STOP to begin. When the cooking is complete, the bagels should be lightly golden on the outside. Serve warm.

All-in-One Toast

Prep time: 10 minutes | Cook time: 10 minutes | Serves 1

1 strip bacon, diced

1 slice 1-inch thick bread

1 egg

Salt and freshly ground black

pepper, to taste

60 ml grated Monterey Jack or Chedday cheese

Preheat the air fryer to 200°C. Air fry the bacon for 3 minutes, shaking the basket once or twice while it cooks. Remove the bacon to a paper towel lined plate and set aside. Use a sharp paring knife to score a large circle in the middle of the slice of bread, cutting halfway through, but not all the way through to the cutting board. Press down on the circle in the center of the bread slice to create an indentation. Transfer the slice of bread, hole side up, to the air fryer basket. Crack the egg into the center of the bread, and season with salt and pepper. Adjust the air fryer temperature to 190°C and air fry for 5 minutes. Sprinkle the grated cheese around the edges of the bread, leaving the center of the yolk uncovered, and top with the cooked bacon. Press the cheese and bacon into the bread lightly to help anchor it to the bread and prevent it from blowing around in the air fryer. Air fry for one or two more minutes, just to melt the cheese and finish cooking the egg. Serve immediately.

Turkey Sausage Breakfast Pizza

Prep time: 15 minutes | Cook time: 24 minutes | Serves 2

4 large eggs, divided

1 tablespoon water

½ teaspoon garlic powder

½ teaspoon onion granules

½ teaspoon dried oregano

2 tablespoons coconut flour

3 tablespoons grated Parmesan cheese

120 ml shredded low-moisture Mozzarella or other melting cheese

1 link cooked turkey sausage, chopped (about 60 g)

2 sun-dried tomatoes, finely chopped

2 sping onions, thinly sliced

Preheat the air fryer to 200°C. Line a cake pan with parchment paper and lightly coat the paper with olive oil. In a large bowl, whisk 2 of the eggs with the water, garlic powder, onion granules, and dried oregano. Add the coconut flour, breaking up any lumps with your hands as you add it to the bowl. Stir the coconut flour into the egg mixture, mixing until smooth. Stir in the Parmesan cheese. Allow the mixture to rest for a few minutes until thick and dough-like. Transfer the mixture to the prepared pan. Use a spatula to spread it evenly and slightly up the sides of the pan. Air fry until the crust is set but still light in color, about 10 minutes. Top with the cheeses, sausage, and sun-dried tomatoes. Break the remaining 2 eggs into a small bowl, then slide them onto the pizza. Return the pizza to the air fryer. Air fry 10 to 14 minutes until the egg whites are set and the yolks are the desired doneness. Top with the scallions and allow to rest for 5 minutes before serving.

Three-Berry Dutch Pancake

Prep time: 10 minutes | Cook time: 12 to 16 minutes | Serves 4

2 egg whites

1 egg

120 ml wholemeal plain flour plus 1 tablespoon cornflour

120 ml semi-skimmed milk

1 teaspoon pure vanilla extract

1 tablespoon unsalted butter, melted

235 ml sliced fresh strawberries

120 ml fresh blueberries

120 ml fresh raspberries

In a medium bowl, use an eggbeater or hand mixer to quickly mix the egg whites, egg, flour, milk, and vanilla until well combined. Use a pastry brush to grease the bottom of a baking pan with the melted butter. Immediately pour in the batter and put the basket back in the fryer. Bake at 165°C for 12 to 16 minutes, or until the pancake is puffed and golden brown. Remove the pan from the air fryer; the pancake will fall. Top with the strawberries, blueberries, and raspberries. Serve immediately.

Smoky Sausage Patties

Prep time: 30 minutes | Cook time: 9 minutes | Serves 8

450 g pork mince	½ teaspoon fennel seeds
1 tablespoon soy sauce or tamari	½ teaspoon dried thyme
1 teaspoon smoked paprika	½ teaspoon freshly ground black pepper
1 teaspoon dried sage	¼ teaspoon cayenne pepper
1 teaspoon sea salt	

In a large bowl, combine the pork, soy sauce, smoked paprika, sage, salt, fennel seeds, thyme, black pepper, and cayenne pepper. Work the meat with your hands until the seasonings are fully incorporated. Shape the mixture into 8 equal-size patties. Using your thumb, make a dent in the center of each patty. Place the patties on a plate and cover with plastic wrap. Refrigerate the patties for at least 30 minutes. Working in batches if necessary, place the patties in a single layer in the air fryer, being careful not to overcrowd them. Set the air fryer to 200°C and air fry for 5 minutes. Flip and cook for about 4 minutes more.

Mexican Breakfast Pepper Rings

Prep time: 5 minutes | Cook time: 10 minutes | Serves 4

Olive oil	4 eggs
1 large red, yellow, or orange pepper, cut into four ¾-inch rings	Salt and freshly ground black pepper, to taste
	2 teaspoons salsa

Preheat the air fryer to 175°C. Lightly spray a baking pan with olive oil. Place 2 bell pepper rings on the pan. Crack one egg into each bell pepper ring. Season with salt and black pepper. Spoon ½ teaspoon of salsa on top of each egg. Place the pan in the air fryer basket. Air fry until the yolk is slightly runny, 5 to 6 minutes or until the yolk is fully cooked, 8 to 10 minutes. Repeat with the remaining 2 pepper rings. Serve hot.

Potatoes Lyonnaise

Prep time: 10 minutes | Cook time: 31 minutes | Serves 4

1 sweet/mild onion, sliced	thick
1 teaspoon butter, melted	1 tablespoon vegetable oil
1 teaspoon brown sugar	Salt and freshly ground black pepper, to taste
2 large white potatoes (about 450 g in total), sliced ½-inch	

Preheat the air fryer to 190°C. Toss the sliced onions, melted butter and brown sugar together in the air fryer basket. Air fry for 8 minutes, shaking the basket occasionally to help the onions cook evenly. While the onions are cooking, bring a saucepan of salted water to a boil on the stovetop. Par-cook the potatoes in boiling water for 3 minutes. Drain the potatoes and pat them dry with a clean kitchen towel. Add the potatoes to the onions in the air fryer basket and drizzle with vegetable oil. Toss to coat the potatoes with the oil and season with salt and freshly ground black pepper. Increase the air fryer temperature to 200°C and air fry for 20 minutes, tossing the vegetables a few times during the cooking time to help the potatoes brown evenly. Season with salt and freshly ground black pepper and serve warm.

Simple Scotch Eggs

Prep time: 5 minutes | Cook time: 25 minutes | Serves 4

4 large hard boiled eggs	8 slices thick-cut bacon
1 (340 g) package pork sausage meat	4 wooden toothpicks, soaked in water for at least 30 minutes

Slice the sausage meat into four parts and place each part into a large circle. Put an egg into each circle and wrap it in the sausage. Put in the refrigerator for 1 hour. Preheat the air fryer to 235°C. Make a cross with two pieces of thick-cut bacon. Put a wrapped egg in the center, fold the bacon over top of the egg, and secure with a toothpick. Air fry in the preheated air fryer for 25 minutes. Serve immediately.

Cinnamon Rolls

Prep time: 10 minutes | Cook time: 20 minutes | Makes 12 rolls

600 ml shredded Mozzarella cheese	½ teaspoon vanilla extract
60 g cream cheese, softened	120 ml icing sugar-style sweetener
235 ml blanched finely ground almond flour	1 tablespoon ground cinnamon

In a large microwave-safe bowl, combine Mozzarella cheese, cream cheese, and flour. Microwave the mixture on high 90 seconds until cheese is melted. Add vanilla extract and sweetener, and mix 2 minutes until a dough forms. Once the dough is cool enough to work with your hands, about 2 minutes, spread it out into a 12 × 4-inch rectangle on ungreased parchment paper. Evenly sprinkle dough with cinnamon. Starting at the long side of the dough, roll lengthwise to form a log. Slice the log into twelve even pieces. Divide rolls between two ungreased round nonstick baking dishes. Place one dish into air fryer basket. Adjust the temperature to 190°C and bake for 10 minutes. Cinnamon rolls will be done when golden around the edges and mostly firm. Repeat with second dish. Allow rolls to cool in dishes 10 minutes before serving.

Poached Eggs on Whole Grain Avocado Toast

Prep time: 5 minutes | Cook time: 7 minutes | Serves 4

Olive oil cooking spray	4 pieces wholegrain bread
4 large eggs	1 avocado
Salt	Red pepper flakes (optional)
Black pepper	

Preheat the air fryer to 160°C. Lightly coat the inside of four small oven-safe ramekins with olive oil cooking spray. Crack one egg into each ramekin, and season with salt and black pepper. Place the ramekins into the air fryer basket. Close and set the timer to 7 minutes. While the eggs are cooking, toast the bread in a toaster. Slice the avocado in half lengthwise, remove the pit, and scoop the flesh into a small bowl. Season with salt, black pepper, and red pepper flakes, if desired. Using a fork, smash the avocado lightly. Spread a quarter of the smashed avocado evenly over each slice of toast. Remove the eggs from the air fryer, and gently spoon one onto each slice of avocado toast before serving.

Apple Cider Doughnut Holes

Prep time: 10 minutes | Cook time: 6 minutes |
Makes 10 mini doughnuts

Doughnut Holes:	apple juice, chilled
350 ml plain flour	1 large egg, lightly beaten
2 tablespoons granulated sugar	Vegetable oil, for brushing
2 teaspoons baking powder	Glaze:
1 teaspoon baking soda	120 ml icing sugar
½ teaspoon coarse or flaky salt	2 tablespoons unsweetened
Pinch of freshly grated nutmeg	applesauce
60 ml plus 2 tablespoons	¼ teaspoon vanilla extract
buttermilk, chilled	Pinch of coarse or flaky salt
2 tablespoons apple cider or	

Make the doughnut holes: In a bowl, whisk together the flour, granulated sugar, baking powder, baking soda, salt, and nutmeg until smooth. Add the buttermilk, cider, and egg and stir with a small rubber spatula or spoon until the dough just comes together. Using a 28 g ice cream scoop or 2 tablespoons, scoop and drop 10 balls of dough into the air fryer basket, spaced evenly apart, and brush the tops lightly with oil. Air fry at 175°C until the doughnut holes are golden brown and fluffy, about 6 minutes. Transfer the doughnut holes to a wire rack to cool completely. Make the glaze: In a small bowl, stir together the powdered sugar, applesauce, vanilla, and salt until smooth. Dip the tops of the doughnuts holes in the glaze, then let stand until the glaze sets before serving. If you're impatient and want warm doughnuts, have the glaze ready to go while the doughnuts cook, then use the glaze as a dipping sauce for the warm doughnuts, fresh out of the air fryer.

Sausage and Egg Breakfast Burrito

Prep time: 5 minutes | Cook time: 30 minutes |
Serves 6

6 eggs	(removed from casings)
Salt and pepper, to taste	120 ml salsa
Cooking oil	6 medium (8-inch) flour tortillas
120 ml chopped red pepper	120 ml shredded Cheddar
120 ml chopped green pepper	cheese
230 g chicken sausage meat	

In a medium bowl, whisk the eggs. Add salt and pepper to taste. Place a skillet on medium-high heat. Spray with cooking oil. Add the eggs. Scramble for 2 to 3 minutes, until the eggs are fluffy. Remove the eggs from the skillet and set aside. If needed, spray the skillet with more oil. Add the chopped red and green bell peppers. Cook for 2 to 3 minutes, until the peppers are soft. Add the sausage meat to the skillet. Break the sausage into smaller pieces using a spatula or spoon. Cook for 3 to 4 minutes, until the sausage is brown. Add the salsa and scrambled eggs. Stir to combine. Remove the skillet from heat. Spoon the mixture evenly onto the tortillas. To form the burritos, fold the sides of each tortilla in toward the middle and then roll up from the bottom. You can secure each burrito with a toothpick. Or you can moisten the outside edge of the tortilla with a small amount of water. I prefer to use a cooking brush, but you can also dab with your fingers. Spray the burritos with cooking oil and place them in the air fryer. Do not stack. Cook the burritos in batches if they do not all fit in the basket. Air fry at 200°C for 8 minutes. Open the air fryer and flip the burritos. Cook for an additional 2 minutes or until crisp. 1If necessary, repeat steps 8 and 9 for the remaining burritos. 1Sprinkle the Cheddar cheese over the burritos. Cool before serving.

Pitta and Pepperoni Pizza

Prep time: 10 minutes | Cook time: 6 minutes | Serves 1

1 teaspoon olive oil	60 ml grated Mozzarella cheese
1 tablespoon pizza sauce	¼ teaspoon garlic powder
1 pitta bread	¼ teaspoon dried oregano
6 pepperoni slices	

Preheat the air fryer to 175°C. Grease the air fryer basket with olive oil. Spread the pizza sauce on top of the pitta bread. Put the pepperoni slices over the sauce, followed by the Mozzarella cheese. Season with garlic powder and oregano. Put the pitta pizza inside the air fryer and place a trivet on top. Bake in the preheated air fryer for 6 minutes and serve.

Broccoli-Mushroom Frittata

Prep time: 10 minutes | Cook time: 20 minutes | Serves 2

1 tablespoon olive oil	½ teaspoon salt
350 ml broccoli florets, finely chopped	¼ teaspoon freshly ground black pepper
120 ml sliced brown mushrooms	6 eggs
60 ml finely chopped onion	60 ml Parmesan cheese

In a nonstick cake pan, combine the olive oil, broccoli, mushrooms, onion, salt, and pepper. Stir until the vegetables are thoroughly coated with oil. Place the cake pan in the air fryer basket and set the air fryer to 200°C. Air fry for 5 minutes until the vegetables soften. Meanwhile, in a medium bowl, whisk the eggs and Parmesan until thoroughly combined. Pour the egg mixture into the pan and shake gently to distribute the vegetables. Air fry for another 15 minutes until the eggs are set. Remove from the air fryer and let sit for 5 minutes to cool slightly. Use a silicone spatula to gently lift the frittata onto a plate before serving.

Gold Avocado

Prep time: 5 minutes | Cook time: 6 minutes | Serves 4

2 large avocados, sliced	120 ml flour
¼ teaspoon paprika	2 eggs, beaten
Salt and ground black pepper, to taste	235 ml bread crumbs

Preheat the air fryer to 200°C. Sprinkle paprika, salt and pepper on the slices of avocado. Lightly coat the avocados with flour. Dredge them in the eggs, before covering with bread crumbs. Transfer to the air fryer and air fry for 6 minutes. Serve warm.

Drop Biscuits

Prep time: 10 minutes | Cook time: 9 to 10 minutes | Serves 5

1 L plain flour	for brushing on the biscuits (optional)
1 tablespoon baking powder	
1 tablespoon sugar (optional)	180 ml buttermilk
1 teaspoon salt	1 to 2 tablespoons oil
6 tablespoons butter, plus more	

In a large bowl, whisk the flour, baking powder, sugar (if using), and salt until blended. Add the butter. Using a pastry cutter or 2 forks, work the dough until pea-size balls of the butter-flour mixture appear. Stir in the buttermilk until the mixture is sticky. Preheat the air fryer to 165°C. Line the air fryer basket with parchment paper and spritz it with oil. Drop the dough by the tablespoonful onto the prepared basket, leaving 1 inch between each, to form 10 biscuits. Bake for 5 minutes. Flip the biscuits and cook for 4 minutes more for a light brown top, or 5 minutes more for a darker biscuit. Brush the tops with melted butter, if desired.

Mississippi Spice Muffins

Prep time: 15 minutes | Cook time: 13 minutes | Makes 12 muffins

1 L plain flour	temperature
1 tablespoon ground cinnamon	475 ml sugar
2 teaspoons baking soda	2 large eggs, lightly beaten
2 teaspoons allspice	475 ml unsweetened applesauce
1 teaspoon ground cloves	60 ml chopped pecans
1 teaspoon salt	1 to 2 tablespoons oil
235 ml (2 sticks) butter, room	

In a large bowl, whisk the flour, cinnamon, baking soda, allspice, cloves, and salt until blended. In another large bowl, combine the butter and sugar. Using an electric mixer, beat the mixture for 2 to 3 minutes until light and fluffy. Add the beaten eggs and stir until blended. Add the flour mixture and applesauce, alternating between the two and blending after each addition. Stir in the pecans. Preheat the air fryer to 165°C. Spritz 12 silicone muffin cups with oil. Pour the batter into the prepared muffin cups, filling each halfway. Place the muffins in the air fryer basket. Air fry for 6 minutes. Shake the basket and air fry for 7 minutes more. The muffins are done when a toothpick inserted into the middle comes out clean.

Cheddar-Ham-Corn Muffins

Prep time: 10 minutes | Cook time: 6 to 8 minutes per batch | Makes 8 muffins

180 ml cornmeal/polenta	120 ml shredded sharp Cheddar cheese
60 ml flour	
1½ teaspoons baking powder	120 ml diced ham
¼ teaspoon salt	8 foil muffin cups, liners removed and sprayed with cooking spray
1 egg, beaten	
2 tablespoons rapeseed oil	
120 ml milk	

Preheat the air fryer to 200°C. In a medium bowl, stir together the cornmeal, flour, baking powder, and salt. Add egg, oil, and milk to dry ingredients and mix well. Stir in shredded cheese and diced ham. Divide batter among the muffin cups. Place 4 filled muffin cups in air fryer basket and bake for 5 minutes. Reduce temperature to 165°C and bake for 1 to 2 minutes or until toothpick inserted in center of muffin comes out clean. Repeat steps 6 and 7 to cook remaining muffins.

Simple Cinnamon Toasts

Prep time: 5 minutes | Cook time: 4 minutes | Serves 4

1 tablespoon salted butter
2 teaspoons ground cinnamon
4 tablespoons sugar

½ teaspoon vanilla extract
10 bread slices

Preheat the air fryer to 190ºC. In a bowl, combine the butter, cinnamon, sugar, and vanilla extract. Spread onto the slices of bread. Put the bread inside the air fryer and bake for 4 minutes or until golden brown. Serve warm.

Classic British Breakfast

Prep time: 5 minutes | Cook time: 25 minutes | Serves 2

235 ml potatoes, sliced and diced
475 ml baked beans
2 eggs

1 tablespoon olive oil
1 sausage
Salt, to taste

Preheat the air fryer to 200ºC and allow to warm. Break the eggs onto a baking dish and sprinkle with salt. Lay the beans on the dish, next to the eggs. In a bowl, coat the potatoes with the olive oil. Sprinkle with salt. Transfer the bowl of potato slices to the air fryer and bake for 10 minutes. Swap out the bowl of potatoes for the dish containing the eggs and beans. Bake for another 10 minutes. Cover the potatoes with parchment paper. Slice up the sausage and throw the slices on top of the beans and eggs. Bake for another 5 minutes. Serve with the potatoes.

Homemade Toaster Pastries

Prep time: 10 minutes | Cook time: 11 minutes | Makes 6 pastries

Oil, for spraying
1 (425 g) package refrigerated piecrust
6 tablespoons jam or preserves of choice

475 ml icing sugar
3 tablespoons milk
1 to 2 tablespoons sprinkles of choice

Preheat the air fryer to 175ºC. Line the air fryer basket with parchment and spray lightly with oil. Cut the piecrust into 12 rectangles, about 3 by 4 inches each. You will need to reroll the dough scraps to get 12 rectangles. Spread 1 tablespoon of jam in the center of 6 rectangles, leaving ¼ inch around the edges. Pour some water into a small bowl. Use your finger to moisten the edge of each rectangle. Top each rectangle with another and use your fingers to press around the edges. Using the tines of a fork, seal the edges of the dough and poke a few holes in the top of each one. Place the pastries in the prepared basket. Air fry for 11 minutes. Let cool completely. In a medium bowl, whisk together the icing sugar and milk. Spread the icing over the tops of the pastries and add sprinkles. Serve immediately.

Chapter 3 Fast and Easy Everyday Favourites

Buttery Sweet Potatoes

Prep time: 5 minutes | Cook time: 10 minutes | Serves 4

2 tablespoons butter, melted
1 tablespoon light brown sugar
2 sweet potatoes, peeled and cut
into ½-inch cubes
Cooking spray

Preheat the air fryer to 200°C. Line the air fryer basket with parchment paper. In a medium bowl, stir together the melted butter and brown sugar until blended. Toss the sweet potatoes in the butter mixture until coated. Place the sweet potatoes on the parchment and spritz with oil. Air fry for 5 minutes. Shake the basket, spritz the sweet potatoes with oil, and air fry for 5 minutes more until they're soft enough to cut with a fork. Serve immediately.

Baked Halloumi with Greek Salsa

Prep timeBaked Halloumi with Greek Salsa

Salsa:
1 small shallot, finely diced
3 garlic cloves, minced
2 tablespoons fresh lemon juice
2 tablespoons extra-virgin olive oil
1 teaspoon freshly cracked black pepper
Pinch of rock salt
120 ml finely diced English cucumber
1 plum tomato, deseeded and
finely diced
2 teaspoons chopped fresh parsley
1 teaspoon snipped fresh dill
1 teaspoon snipped fresh oregano
Cheese:
227 g Halloumi cheese, sliced into ½-inch-thick pieces
1 tablespoon extra-virgin olive oil

Preheat the air fryer to 190°C. For the salsa: Combine the shallot, garlic, lemon juice, olive oil, pepper, and salt in a medium bowl. Add the cucumber, tomato, parsley, dill, and oregano. Toss gently to combine; set aside. For the cheese: Place the cheese slices in a medium bowl. Drizzle with the olive oil. Toss gently to coat. Arrange the cheese in a single layer in the air fryer basket. Bake for 6 minutes. Divide the cheese among four serving plates. Top with the salsa and serve immediately.

Beef Bratwursts

Prep time: 5 minutes | Cook time: 15 minutes | Serves 4

4 (85 g) beef bratwursts

Preheat the air fryer to 190°C. Place the beef bratwursts in the air fryer basket and air fry for 15 minutes, turning once halfway through. Serve hot.

Simple and Easy Croutons

Prep time: 5 minutes | Cook time: 8 minutes | Serves 4

2 slices bread
1 tablespoon olive oil
Hot soup, for serving

Preheat the air fryer to 200°C. Cut the slices of bread into medium-size chunks. Brush the air fryer basket with the oil. Place the chunks inside and air fry for at least 8 minutes. Serve with hot soup.

Peppery Brown Rice Fritters

Prep time: 10 minutes | Cook time: 8 to 10 minutes | Serves 4

1 (284 g) bag frozen cooked brown rice, thawed
1 egg
3 tablespoons brown rice flour
80 ml finely grated carrots
80 ml minced red pepper
2 tablespoons minced fresh basil
3 tablespoons grated Parmesan cheese
2 teaspoons olive oil

Preheat the air fryer to 190°C. In a small bowl, combine the thawed rice, egg, and flour and mix to blend. Stir in the carrots, pepper, basil, and Parmesan cheese. Form the mixture into 8 fritters and drizzle with the olive oil. Put the fritters carefully into the air fryer basket. Air fry for 8 to 10 minutes, or until the fritters are golden brown and cooked through. Serve immediately.

Cheesy Baked Grits

Prep time: 10 minutes | Cook time: 12 minutes | Serves 6

180 ml hot water
2 (28 g) packages instant grits
1 large egg, beaten
1 tablespoon butter, melted
2 cloves garlic, minced
½ to 1 teaspoon red pepper flakes
235 ml shredded Cheddar cheese or jalapeño Jack cheese

Preheat the air fryer to 200ºC. In a baking pan, combine the water, grits, egg, butter, garlic, and red pepper flakes. Stir until well combined. Stir in the shredded cheese. Place the pan in the air fryer basket and air fry for 12 minutes, or until the grits have cooked through and a knife inserted near the centre comes out clean. Let stand for 5 minutes before serving.

Corn Fritters

Prep time: 15 minutes | Cook time: 8 minutes | Serves 6

235 ml self-raising flour
1 tablespoon sugar
1 teaspoon salt
1 large egg, lightly beaten
60 ml buttermilk
180 ml corn kernels
60 ml minced onion
Cooking spray

Preheat the air fryer to 175ºC. Line the air fryer basket with parchment paper. In a medium bowl, whisk the flour, sugar, and salt until blended. Stir in the egg and buttermilk. Add the corn and minced onion. Mix well. Shape the corn fritter batter into 12 balls. Place the fritters on the parchment and spritz with oil. Bake for 4 minutes. Flip the fritters, spritz them with oil, and bake for 4 minutes more until firm and lightly browned. Serve immediately.

Cheesy Potato Patties

Prep time: 5 minutes | Cook time: 10 minutes | Serves 8

900 g white potatoes
120 ml finely chopped spring onions
½ teaspoon freshly ground black pepper, or more to taste
1 tablespoon fine sea salt
½ teaspoon hot paprika
475 ml shredded Colby or Monterey Jack cheese
60 ml rapeseed oil
235 ml crushed crackers

Preheat the air fryer to 180ºC. Boil the potatoes until soft. Dry them off and peel them before mashing thoroughly, leaving no lumps. Combine the mashed potatoes with spring onions, pepper, salt, paprika, and cheese. Mould the mixture into balls with your hands and press with your palm to flatten them into patties. In a shallow dish, combine the rapeseed oil and crushed crackers. Coat the patties in the crumb mixture. Bake the patties for about 10 minutes, in multiple batches if necessary. Serve hot.

Cheesy Chilli Toast

Prep time: 5 minutes | Cook time: 5 minutes | Serves 1

2 tablespoons grated Parmesan cheese
2 tablespoons grated Mozzarella cheese
2 teaspoons salted butter, at
room temperature
10 to 15 thin slices serrano chilli or jalapeño
2 slices sourdough bread
½ teaspoon black pepper

Preheat the air fryer to 165ºC. In a small bowl, stir together the Parmesan, Mozzarella, butter, and chillies. Spread half the mixture onto one side of each slice of bread. Sprinkle with the pepper. Place the slices, cheese-side up, in the air fryer basket. Bake for 5 minutes, or until the cheese has melted and started to brown slightly. Serve immediately.

Herb-Roasted Veggies

Prep time: 10 minutes | Cook time: 14 to 18 minutes | Serves 4

1 red pepper, sliced
1 (230 g) package sliced mushrooms
235 ml green beans, cut into 2-inch pieces
80 ml diced red onion
3 garlic cloves, sliced
1 teaspoon olive oil
½ teaspoon dried basil
½ teaspoon dried tarragon

Preheat the air fryer to 175ºC. In a medium bowl, mix the red pepper, mushrooms, green beans, red onion, and garlic. Drizzle with the olive oil. Toss to coat. Add the herbs and toss again. Place the vegetables in the air fryer basket. Roast for 14 to 18 minutes, or until tender. Serve immediately.

Air Fried Tortilla Chips

Prep time: 5 minutes | Cook time: 10 minutes | Serves 4

4 six-inch corn tortillas, cut in half and slice into thirds
1 tablespoon rapeseed oil
¼ teaspoon rock salt
Cooking spray

Preheat the air fryer to 180ºC. Spritz the air fryer basket with cooking spray. On a clean work surface, brush the tortilla chips with rapeseed oil, then transfer the chips in the preheated air fryer. Air fry for 10 minutes or until crunchy and lightly browned. Shake the basket and sprinkle with salt halfway through the cooking time. Transfer the chips onto a plate lined with paper towels. Serve immediately.

Spinach and Carrot Balls

Prep time: 10 minutes | Cook time: 10 minutes | Serves 4

2 slices toasted bread	1 teaspoon minced garlic
1 carrot, peeled and grated	1 teaspoon salt
1 package fresh spinach, blanched and chopped	½ teaspoon black pepper
½ onion, chopped	1 tablespoon Engevita yeast flakes
1 egg, beaten	1 tablespoon flour
½ teaspoon garlic powder	

Preheat the air fryer to 200°C. In a food processor, pulse the toasted bread to form breadcrumbs. Transfer into a shallow dish or bowl. In a bowl, mix together all the other ingredients. Use your hands to shape the mixture into small-sized balls. Roll the balls in the breadcrumbs, ensuring to cover them well. Put in the air fryer basket and air fry for 10 minutes. Serve immediately.

Easy Devils on Horseback

Prep time: 5 minutes | Cook time: 7 minutes | Serves 12

24 small pitted prunes (128 g)	8 slices centre-cut bacon, cut crosswise into thirds
60 ml crumbled blue cheese, divided	

Preheat the air fryer to 200°C. Halve the prunes lengthwise, but don't cut them all the way through. Place ½ teaspoon of cheese in the centre of each prune. Wrap a piece of bacon around each prune and secure the bacon with a toothpick. Working in batches, arrange a single layer of the prunes in the air fryer basket. Air fry for about 7 minutes, flipping halfway, until the bacon is cooked through and crisp. Let cool slightly and serve warm.

Air Fried Courgette Sticks

Prep time: 5 minutes | Cook time: 20 minutes | Serves 4

1 medium courgette, cut into 48 sticks	1 tablespoon melted margarine
60 ml seasoned breadcrumbs	Cooking spray

Preheat the air fryer to 180°C. Spritz the air fryer basket with cooking spray and set aside. In 2 different shallow bowls, add the seasoned breadcrumbs and the margarine. One by one, dredge the courgette sticks into the margarine, then roll in the breadcrumbs to coat evenly. Arrange the crusted sticks on a plate. Place the courgette sticks in the prepared air fryer basket. Work in two batches to avoid overcrowding. Air fry for 10 minutes, or until golden brown and crispy. Shake the basket halfway through to cook evenly. When the cooking time is over, transfer the fries to a wire rack. Rest for 5 minutes and serve warm.

Crunchy Fried Okra

Prep time: 5 minutes | Cook time: 8 to 10 minutes | Serves 4

235 ml self-raising yellow cornmeal (alternatively add 1 tablespoon baking powder to cornmeal)	1 teaspoon salt
1 teaspoon Italian-style seasoning	½ teaspoon freshly ground black pepper
1 teaspoon paprika	2 large eggs, beaten
	475 ml okra slices
	Cooking spray

Preheat the air fryer to 200°C. Line the air fryer basket with parchment paper. In a shallow bowl, whisk the cornmeal, Italian-style seasoning, paprika, salt, and pepper until blended. Place the beaten eggs in a second shallow bowl. Add the okra to the beaten egg and stir to coat. Add the egg and okra mixture to the cornmeal mixture and stir until coated. Place the okra on the parchment and spritz it with oil. Air fry for 4 minutes. Shake the basket, spritz the okra with oil, and air fry for 4 to 6 minutes more until lightly browned and crispy. Serve immediately.

Easy Roasted Asparagus

Prep time: 5 minutes | Cook time: 6 minutes | Serves 4

450 g asparagus, trimmed and halved crosswise	Salt and pepper, to taste
1 teaspoon extra-virgin olive oil	Lemon wedges, for serving

Preheat the air fryer to 200°C. Toss the asparagus with the oil, ⅛ teaspoon salt, and ⅛ teaspoon pepper in bowl. Transfer to air fryer basket. Place the basket in air fryer and roast for 6 to 8 minutes, or until tender and bright green, tossing halfway through cooking. Season with salt and pepper and serve with lemon wedges.

Air Fried Broccoli

Prep time: 5 minutes | Cook time: 6 minutes | Serves 1

4 egg yolks	Salt and pepper, to taste
60 ml butter, melted	475 ml broccoli florets
475 ml coconut flour	

Preheat the air fryer to 200°C. In a bowl, whisk the egg yolks and melted butter together. Throw in the coconut flour, salt and pepper, then stir again to combine well. Dip each broccoli floret into the mixture and place in the air fryer basket. Air fry for 6 minutes in batches if necessary. Take care when removing them from the air fryer and serve immediately.

Scalloped Veggie Mix

Prep time: 10 minutes | Cook time: 15 minutes | Serves 4

1 Yukon Gold or other small white potato, thinly sliced	60 ml minced onion
1 small sweet potato, peeled and thinly sliced	3 garlic cloves, minced
1 medium carrot, thinly sliced	180 ml 2 percent milk
	2 tablespoons cornflour
	½ teaspoon dried thyme

Preheat the air fryer to 190ºC. In a baking pan, layer the potato, sweet potato, carrot, onion, and garlic. In a small bowl, whisk the milk, cornflour, and thyme until blended. Pour the milk mixture evenly over the vegetables in the pan. Bake for 15 minutes. Check the casserole—it should be golden brown on top, and the vegetables should be tender. Serve immediately.

Baked Cheese Sandwich

Prep time: 5 minutes | Cook time: 8 minutes | Serves 2

2 tablespoons mayonnaise	8 slices hot capicola or prosciutto
4 thick slices sourdough bread	
4 thick slices Brie cheese	

Preheat the air fryer to 175ºC. Spread the mayonnaise on one side of each slice of bread. Place 2 slices of bread in the air fryer basket, mayonnaise-side down. Place the slices of Brie and capicola on the bread and cover with the remaining two slices of bread, mayonnaise-side up. Bake for 8 minutes, or until the cheese has melted. Serve immediately.

Traditional Queso Fundido

Prep time: 10 minutes | Cook time: 25 minutes | Serves 4

110 g fresh Mexican (or Spanish if unavailable) chorizo, casings removed	475 ml shredded Oaxaca or Mozzarella cheese
1 medium onion, chopped	120 ml half-and-half (60 ml whole milk and 60 ml cream combined)
3 cloves garlic, minced	
235 ml chopped tomato	Celery sticks or tortilla chips, for serving
2 jalapeños, deseeded and diced	
2 teaspoons ground cumin	

Preheat the air fryer to 200ºC. In a baking pan, combine the chorizo, onion, garlic, tomato, jalapeños, and cumin. Stir to combine. Place the pan in the air fryer basket. Air fry for 15 minutes, or until the sausage is cooked, stirring halfway through the cooking time to break up the sausage. Add the cheese and half-and-half; stir to combine. Air fry for 10 minutes, or until the cheese has melted. Serve with celery sticks or tortilla chips.

Purple Potato Chips with Rosemary

Prep time: 10 minutes | Cook time: 9 to 14 minutes | Serves 6

235 ml Greek yoghurt	miniature potatoes
2 chipotle chillies, minced	1 teaspoon olive oil
2 tablespoons adobo or chipotle sauce	2 teaspoons minced fresh rosemary leaves
1 teaspoon paprika	⅛ teaspoon cayenne pepper
1 tablespoon lemon juice	¼ teaspoon coarse sea salt
10 purple fingerling or	

Preheat the air fryer to 200ºC. In a medium bowl, combine the yoghurt, minced chillies, adobo sauce, paprika, and lemon juice. Mix well and refrigerate. Wash the potatoes and dry them with paper towels. Slice the potatoes lengthwise, as thinly as possible. You can use a mandoline, a vegetable peeler, or a very sharp knife. Combine the potato slices in a medium bowl and drizzle with the olive oil; toss to coat. Air fry the chips, in batches, in the air fryer basket, for 9 to 14 minutes. Use tongs to gently rearrange the chips halfway during cooking time. Sprinkle the chips with the rosemary, cayenne pepper, and sea salt. Serve with the chipotle sauce for dipping.

Beery and Crunchy Onion Rings

Prep time: 10 minutes | Cook time: 16 minutes | Serves 2 to 4

160 ml plain flour	180 ml beer
1 teaspoon paprika	350 ml breadcrumbs
½ teaspoon bicarbonate of soda	1 tablespoons olive oil
1 teaspoon salt	1 large Vidalia or sweet onion, peeled and sliced into ½-inch rings
½ teaspoon freshly ground black pepper	
1 egg, beaten	Cooking spray

Preheat the air fryer to 180ºC. Spritz the air fryer basket with cooking spray. Combine the flour, paprika, bicarbonate of soda, salt, and ground black pepper in a bowl. Stir to mix well. Combine the egg and beer in a separate bowl. Stir to mix well. Make a well in the centre of the flour mixture, then pour the egg mixture in the well. Stir to mix everything well. Pour the breadcrumbs and olive oil in a shallow plate. Stir to mix well. Dredge the onion rings gently into the flour and egg mixture, then shake the excess off and put into the plate of breadcrumbs. Flip to coat both sides well. Arrange the onion rings in the preheated air fryer. Air fry in batches for 16 minutes or until golden brown and crunchy. Flip the rings and put the bottom rings to the top halfway through. Serve immediately.

Cheesy Jalapeño Cornbread

Prep timeCheesy Jalapeño Cornbread

160 ml cornmeal	180 ml whole milk
80 ml plain flour	1 large egg, beaten
¾ teaspoon baking powder	1 jalapeño pepper, thinly sliced
2 tablespoons margarine, melted	80 ml shredded extra mature Cheddar cheese
½ teaspoon rock salt	Cooking spray
1 tablespoon granulated sugar	

Preheat the air fryer to 150°C. Spritz the air fryer basket with cooking spray. Combine all the ingredients in a large bowl. Stir to mix well. Pour the mixture in a baking pan. Arrange the pan in the preheated air fryer. Bake for 20 minutes or until a toothpick inserted in the centre of the bread comes out clean. When the cooking is complete, remove the baking pan from the air fryer and allow the bread to cool for a few minutes before slicing to serve.

Air Fried Shishito Peppers

Prep time: 5 minutes | Cook time: 5 minutes | Serves 4

230 g shishito or Padron peppers (about 24)	Coarse sea salt, to taste
1 tablespoon olive oil	Lemon wedges, for serving
	Cooking spray

Preheat the air fryer to 200°C. Spritz the air fryer basket with cooking spray. Toss the peppers with olive oil in a large bowl to coat well. Arrange the peppers in the preheated air fryer. Air fryer for 5 minutes or until blistered and lightly charred. Shake the basket and sprinkle the peppers with salt halfway through the cooking time. Transfer the peppers onto a plate and squeeze the lemon wedges on top before serving.

Baked Chorizo Scotch Eggs

Prep timeBaked Chorizo Scotch Eggs

450 g Mexican chorizo or other seasoned sausage meat	1 tablespoon water
4 soft-boiled eggs plus 1 raw egg	120 ml plain flour
	235 ml panko breadcrumbs
	Cooking spray

Divide the chorizo into 4 equal portions. Flatten each portion into a disc. Place a soft-boiled egg in the centre of each disc. Wrap the chorizo around the egg, encasing it completely. Place the encased eggs on a plate and chill for at least 30 minutes. Preheat the air fryer to 180°C. Beat the raw egg with 1 tablespoon of water. Place the flour on a small plate and the panko on a second plate. Working with 1 egg at a time, roll the encased egg in the flour, then dip it in the egg mixture. Dredge the egg in the panko and place on a plate. Repeat with the remaining eggs. Spray the eggs with oil and place in the air fryer basket. Bake for 10 minutes. Turn and bake for an additional 5 to 10 minutes, or until browned and crisp on all sides. Serve immediately.

Air Fried Butternut Squash with Chopped Hazelnuts

Prep time: 10 minutes | Cook time: 20 minutes | Makes 700 ml

2 tablespoons whole hazelnuts	¼ teaspoon freshly ground black pepper
700 ml butternut squash, peeled, deseeded, and cubed	2 teaspoons olive oil
¼ teaspoon rock salt	Cooking spray

Preheat the air fryer to 150°C. Spritz the air fryer basket with cooking spray. Arrange the hazelnuts in the preheated air fryer. Air fry for 3 minutes or until soft. Chopped the hazelnuts roughly and transfer to a small bowl. Set aside. Set the air fryer temperature to 180°C. Spritz with cooking spray. Put the butternut squash in a large bowl, then sprinkle with salt and pepper and drizzle with olive oil. Toss to coat well. Transfer the squash in the air fryer. Air fry for 20 minutes or until the squash is soft. Shake the basket halfway through the frying time. When the frying is complete, transfer the squash onto a plate and sprinkle with chopped hazelnuts before serving.

Beetroot Salad with Lemon Vinaigrette

Prep time: 10 minutes | Cook time: 12 to 15 minutes | Serves 4

6 medium red and golden beetroots, peeled and sliced	Cooking spray
1 teaspoon olive oil	Vinaigrette:
¼ teaspoon rock salt	2 teaspoons olive oil
120 ml crumbled feta cheese	2 tablespoons chopped fresh chives
2 L mixed greens	Juice of 1 lemon

Preheat the air fryer to 180°C. In a large bowl, toss the beetroots, olive oil, and rock salt. Spray the air fryer basket with cooking spray, then place the beetroots in the basket and air fry for 12 to 15 minutes or until tender. While the beetroots cook, make the vinaigrette in a large bowl by whisking together the olive oil, lemon juice, and chives. Remove the beetroots from the air fryer, toss in the vinaigrette, and allow to cool for 5 minutes. Add the feta and serve on top of the mixed greens.

Simple Pea Delight

Prep time: 5 minutes | Cook time: 15 minutes | Serves 2 to 4

235 ml flour
1 teaspoon baking powder
3 eggs
235 ml coconut milk
235 ml soft white cheese

3 tablespoons pea protein
120 ml chicken or turkey strips
Pinch of sea salt
235 ml Mozzarella cheese

Preheat the air fryer to 200°C. In a large bowl, mix all ingredients together using a large wooden spoon. Spoon equal amounts of the mixture into muffin cups and bake for 15 minutes. Serve immediately.

Bacon Pinwheels

Prep time: 10 minutes | Cook time: 10 minutes | Makes 8 pinwheels

1 sheet puff pastry
2 tablespoons maple syrup
60 ml brown sugar

8 slices bacon
Ground black pepper, to taste
Cooking spray

Preheat the air fryer to 180°C. Spritz the air fryer basket with cooking spray. Roll the puff pastry into a 10-inch square with a rolling pin on a clean work surface, then cut the pastry into 8 strips. Brush the strips with maple syrup and sprinkle with sugar, leaving a 1-inch far end uncovered. Arrange each slice of bacon on each strip, leaving a ⅛-inch length of bacon hang over the end close to you. Sprinkle with black pepper. From the end close to you, roll the strips into pinwheels, then dab the uncovered end with water and seal the rolls. Arrange the pinwheels in the preheated air fryer and spritz with cooking spray. Air fry for 10 minutes or until golden brown. Flip the pinwheels halfway through. Serve immediately.

Sweet Corn and Carrot Fritters

Prep time: 10 minutes | Cook time: 8 to 11 minutes | Serves 4

Prep time: 10 minutes | Cook time: 8 to 11 minutes | Serves 4

Preheat the air fryer to 175°C. Place the grated carrot in a colander and press down to squeeze out any excess moisture. Dry it with a paper towel. Combine the carrots with the remaining ingredients. Mould 1 tablespoon of the mixture into a ball and press it down with your hand or a spoon to flatten it. Repeat until the rest of the mixture is used up. Spritz the balls with cooking spray. Arrange in the air fryer basket, taking care not to overlap any balls. Bake for 8 to 11 minutes, or until they're firm. Serve warm.

Chapter 4 Snacks and Appetisers

Crispy Mozzarella Sticks

Prep time: 8 minutes | Cook time: 5 minutes | Serves 4

120 ml plain flour	½ teaspoon garlic salt
1 egg, beaten	6 Mozzarella sticks, halved
120 ml panko breadcrumbs	crosswise
120 ml grated Parmesan cheese	Olive oil spray
1 teaspoon Italian seasoning	

Put the flour in a small bowl. Put the beaten egg in another small bowl. In a medium bowl, stir together the panko, Parmesan cheese, Italian seasoning, and garlic salt. Roll a Mozzarella-stick half in the flour, dip it into the egg, and then roll it in the panko mixture to coat. Press the coating lightly to make sure the breadcrumbs stick to the cheese. Repeat with the remaining 11 Mozzarella sticks. Insert the crisper plate into the basket and the basket into the unit. Preheat the unit by selecting AIR FRY, setting the temperature to 200°C, and setting the time to 3 minutes. Select START/STOP to begin. Once the unit is preheated, spray the crisper plate with olive oil and place a parchment paper liner in the basket. Place the Mozzarella sticks into the basket and lightly spray them with olive oil. Select AIR FRY, set the temperature to 200°C, and set the time to 5 minutes. Select START/STOP to begin. When the cooking is complete, the Mozzarella sticks should be golden and crispy. Let the sticks stand for 1 minute before transferring them to a serving plate. Serve warm.

Golden Onion Rings

Prep time: 15 minutes | Cook time: 14 minutes per batch | Serves 4

1 large white onion, peeled and cut into ½ to ¾-inch-thick slices (about 475 ml)	black pepper, divided
	¾ teaspoon granulated garlic, divided
120 ml semi-skimmed milk	355 ml wholemeal
240 ml wholemeal pastry flour, or plain flour	breadcrumbs, or gluten-free breadcrumbs
2 tablespoons cornflour	Cooking oil spray (coconut, sunflower, or safflower)
¾ teaspoon sea salt, divided	Ketchup, for serving (optional)
½ teaspoon freshly ground	

Carefully separate the onion slices into rings—a gentle touch is important here. Place the milk in a shallow bowl and set aside. Make the first breading: In a medium bowl, stir together the flour, cornflour, ¼ teaspoon of salt, ¼ teaspoon of pepper, and ¼ teaspoon of granulated garlic. Set aside. Make the second breading: In a separate medium bowl, stir together the breadcrumbs with the remaining ½ teaspoon of salt, the remaining ½ teaspoon of garlic, and the remaining ½ teaspoon of pepper. Set aside. Insert the crisper plate into the basket and the basket into the unit. Preheat the unit by selecting AIR FRY, setting the temperature to 200°C, and setting the time to 3 minutes. Select START/STOP to begin. Once the unit is preheated, spray the crisper plate and the basket with cooking oil. To make the onion rings, dip one ring into the milk and into the first breading mixture. Dip the ring into the milk again and back into the first breading mixture, coating thoroughly. Dip the ring into the milk one last time and then into the second breading mixture, coating thoroughly. Gently lay the onion ring in the basket. Repeat with additional rings and, as you place them into the basket, do not overlap them too much. Once all the onion rings are in the basket, generously spray the tops with cooking oil. Select AIR FRY, set the temperature to 200°C, and set the time to 14 minutes. Insert the basket into the unit. Select START/STOP to begin. After 4 minutes, open the unit and spray the rings generously with cooking oil. Close the unit to resume cooking. After 3 minutes, remove the basket and spray the onion rings again. Remove the rings, turn them over, and place them back into the basket. Generously spray them again with oil. Reinsert the basket to resume cooking. After 4 minutes, generously spray the rings with oil one last time. Resume cooking for the remaining 3 minutes, or until the onion rings are very crunchy and brown. 1When the cooking is complete, serve the hot rings with ketchup, or other sauce of choice.

Spicy Chicken Bites

Prep time: 10 minutes | Cook time: 10 to 12 minutes | Makes 30 bites

227 g boneless and skinless chicken thighs, cut into 30 pieces	¼ teaspoon rock salt
	2 tablespoons hot sauce
	Cooking spray

Preheat the air fryer to 200°C. Spray the air fryer basket with cooking spray and season the chicken bites with the rock salt, then place in the basket and air fry for 10 to 12 minutes or until crispy. While the chicken bites cook, pour the hot sauce into a large bowl. Remove the bites and add to the sauce bowl, tossing to coat. Serve warm.

Cheesy Courgette Tots

Prep time: 15 minutes | Cook time: 6 minutes | Serves 8

2 medium courgette (about 340 g), shredded
1 large egg, whisked
120 ml grated pecorino Romano cheese
120 ml panko breadcrumbs
¼ teaspoon black pepper
1 clove garlic, minced
Cooking spray

Using your hands, squeeze out as much liquid from the courgette as possible. In a large bowl, mix the courgette with the remaining ingredients except the oil until well incorporated. Make the courgette tots: Use a spoon or cookie scoop to place tablespoonfuls of the courgette mixture onto a lightly floured cutting board and form into 1-inch logs. Preheat air fryer to 190ºC. Spritz the air fryer basket with cooking spray. Place the tots in the basket. You may need to cook in batches to avoid overcrowding. Air fry for 6 minutes until golden brown. Remove from the basket to a serving plate and repeat with the remaining courgette tots. Serve immediately.

Authentic Scotch Eggs

Prep time: 15 minutes | Cook time: 11 to 13 minutes | Serves 6

680 g bulk lean chicken or turkey sausage
3 raw eggs, divided
355 ml dried breadcrumbs,
divided
120 ml plain flour
6 hardboiled eggs, peeled
Cooking oil spray

In a large bowl, combine the chicken sausage, 1 raw egg, and 120 ml of breadcrumbs and mix well. Divide the mixture into 6 pieces and flatten each into a long oval. In a shallow bowl, beat the remaining 2 raw eggs. Place the flour in a small bowl. Place the remaining 240 ml of breadcrumbs in a second small bowl. Roll each hardboiled egg in the flour and wrap one of the chicken sausage pieces around each egg to encircle it completely. One at a time, roll the encased eggs in the flour, dip in the beaten eggs, and finally dip in the breadcrumbs to coat. Insert the crisper plate into the basket and the basket into the unit. Preheat the unit by selecting AIR FRY, setting the temperature to 190ºC, and setting the time to 3 minutes. Select START/STOP to begin. Once the unit is preheated, spray the crisper plate with cooking oil. Place the eggs in a single layer into the basket and spray them with oil. Select AIR FRY, set the temperature to 190ºC, and set the time to 13 minutes. Select START/STOP to begin. 1After about 6 minutes, use tongs to turn the eggs and spray them with more oil. Resume cooking for 5 to 7 minutes more, or until the chicken is thoroughly cooked and the Scotch eggs are browned. 1When the cooking is complete, serve warm.

Chilli-Brined Fried Calamari

Prep time: 20 minutes | Cook time: 8 minutes | Serves 2

1 (227 g) jar sweet or hot pickled cherry peppers
227 g calamari bodies and tentacles, bodies cut into ½-inch-wide rings
1 lemon
475 ml plain flour
Rock salt and freshly ground
black pepper, to taste
3 large eggs, lightly beaten
Cooking spray
120 ml mayonnaise
1 teaspoon finely chopped rosemary
1 garlic clove, minced

Drain the pickled pepper brine into a large bowl and tear the peppers into bite-size strips. Add the pepper strips and calamari to the brine and let stand in the refrigerator for 20 minutes or up to 2 hours. Grate the lemon zest into a large bowl then whisk in the flour and season with salt and pepper. Dip the calamari and pepper strips in the egg, then toss them in the flour mixture until fully coated. Spray the calamari and peppers liberally with cooking spray, then transfer half to the air fryer. Air fry at 200ºC, shaking the basket halfway into cooking, until the calamari is cooked through and golden brown, about 8 minutes. Transfer to a plate and repeat with the remaining pieces. In a small bowl, whisk together the mayonnaise, rosemary, and garlic. Squeeze half the zested lemon to get 1 tablespoon of juice and stir it into the sauce. Season with salt and pepper. Cut the remaining zested lemon half into 4 small wedges and serve alongside the calamari, peppers, and sauce.

Sausage Balls with Cheese

Prep time: 10 minutes | Cook time: 10 to 11 minutes | Serves 8

340 g mild sausage meat
355 ml baking mix
240 ml shredded mild Cheddar cheese
85 g soft white cheese, at room temperature
1 to 2 tablespoons olive oil

Preheat the air fryer to 165ºC. Line the air fryer basket with parchment paper. Mix together the ground sausage, baking mix, Cheddar cheese, and soft white cheese in a large bowl and stir to incorporate. Divide the sausage mixture into 16 equal portions and roll them into 1-inch balls with your hands. Arrange the sausage balls on the parchment, leaving space between each ball. You may need to work in batches to avoid overcrowding. Brush the sausage balls with the olive oil. Bake for 10 to 11 minutes, shaking the basket halfway through, or until the balls are firm and lightly browned on both sides. Remove from the basket to a plate and repeat with the remaining balls. Serve warm.

Pickle Chips

Prep time: 30 minutes | Cook time: 12 minutes | Serves 4

Oil, for spraying
475 ml sliced dill or sweet
pickles, drained
240 ml buttermilk

475 ml plain flour
2 large eggs, beaten
475 ml panko breadcrumbs
¼ teaspoon salt

Line the air fryer basket with parchment and spray lightly with oil. In a shallow bowl, combine the pickles and buttermilk and let soak for at least 1 hour, then drain. Place the flour, beaten eggs, and breadcrumbs in separate bowls. Coat each pickle chip lightly in the flour, dip in the eggs, and dredge in the breadcrumbs. Be sure each one is evenly coated. Place the pickle chips in the prepared basket, sprinkle with the salt, and spray lightly with oil. You may need to work in batches, depending on the size of your air fryer. Air fry at 200°C for 5 minutes, flip, and cook for another 5 to 7 minutes, or until crispy. Serve hot.

Veggie Salmon Nachos

Prep time: 10 minutes | Cook time: 9 to 12 minutes | Serves 6

57 g baked no-salt corn tortilla
chips
1 (142 g) baked salmon fillet,
flaked
120 ml canned low-salt black
beans, rinsed and drained

1 red pepper, chopped
120 ml grated carrot
1 jalapeño pepper, minced
80 ml shredded low-salt low-fat
Swiss cheese
1 tomato, chopped

Preheat the air fryer to 180°C. In a baking pan, layer the tortilla chips. Top with the salmon, black beans, red pepper, carrot, jalapeño, and Swiss cheese. Bake in the air fryer for 9 to 12 minutes, or until the cheese is melted and starts to brown. Top with the tomato and serve.

Garlicky and Cheesy French Fries

Prep time: 5 minutes | Cook time: 20 to 25 minutes | Serves 4

3 medium russet or Maris Piper
potatoes, rinsed, dried, and cut
into thin wedges or classic fry
shapes
2 tablespoons extra-virgin olive
oil
1 tablespoon granulated garlic

80 ml grated Parmesan cheese
½ teaspoon salt
¼ teaspoon freshly ground
black pepper
Cooking oil spray
2 tablespoons finely chopped
fresh parsley (optional)

In a large bowl combine the potato wedges or fries and the olive oil. Toss to coat. Sprinkle the potatoes with the granulated garlic, Parmesan cheese, salt, and pepper, and toss again. Insert the crisper plate into the basket and the basket into the unit. Preheat the unit by selecting AIR FRY, setting the temperature to 200°C, and setting the time to 3 minutes. Select START/STOP to begin. Once the unit is preheated, spray the crisper plate with cooking oil. Place the potatoes into the basket. Select AIR FRY, set the temperature to 200°C, and set the time to 20 to 25 minutes. Select START/STOP to begin. After about 10 minutes, remove the basket and shake it so the fries at the bottom come up to the top. Reinsert the basket to resume cooking. When the cooking is complete, top the fries with the parsley (if using) and serve hot.

Garlic Edamame

Prep time: 5 minutes | Cook time: 10 minutes | Serves 4

Olive oil
1 (454 g) bag frozen edamame
in pods
½ teaspoon salt
½ teaspoon garlic salt

¼ teaspoon freshly ground
black pepper
½ teaspoon red pepper flakes
(optional)

Spray the air fryer basket lightly with olive oil. In a medium bowl, add the frozen edamame and lightly spray with olive oil. Toss to coat. In a small bowl, mix together the salt, garlic salt, black pepper, and red pepper flakes (if using). Add the mixture to the edamame and toss until evenly coated. Place half the edamame in the air fryer basket. Do not overfill the basket. Air fry at 190°C for 5 minutes. Shake the basket and cook until the edamame is starting to brown and get crispy, 3 to 5 more minutes. Repeat with the remaining edamame and serve immediately.

Rosemary-Garlic Shoestring Fries

Prep time: 5 minutes | Cook time: 18 minutes | Serves 2

1 large russet or Maris Piper
potato (about 340 g), scrubbed
clean, and julienned
1 tablespoon vegetable oil
Leaves from 1 sprig fresh

rosemary
Rock salt and freshly ground
black pepper, to taste
1 garlic clove, thinly sliced
Flaky sea salt, for serving

Preheat the air fryer to 200°C. Place the julienned potatoes in a large colander and rinse under cold running water until the water runs clear. Spread the potatoes out on a double-thick layer of paper towels and pat dry. In a large bowl, combine the potatoes, oil, and rosemary. Season with rock salt and pepper and toss to coat evenly. Place the potatoes in the air fryer and air fry for 18 minutes, shaking the basket every 5 minutes and adding the garlic in the last 5 minutes of cooking, or until the fries are golden brown and crisp. Transfer the fries to a plate and sprinkle with flaky sea salt while they're hot. Serve immediately.

Rumaki

Prep time: 30 minutes | Cook time: 10 to 12 minutes per batch | Makes about 24 rumaki

283 g raw chicken livers
1 can sliced water chestnuts, drained

60 ml low-salt teriyaki sauce
12 slices turkey bacon

Cut livers into 1½-inch pieces, trimming out tough veins as you slice. Place livers, water chestnuts, and teriyaki sauce in small container with lid. If needed, add another tablespoon of teriyaki sauce to make sure livers are covered. Refrigerate for 1 hour. When ready to cook, cut bacon slices in half crosswise. Wrap 1 piece of liver and 1 slice of water chestnut in each bacon strip. Secure with toothpick. When you have wrapped half of the livers, place them in the air fryer basket in a single layer. Air fry at 200ºC for 10 to 12 minutes, until liver is done, and bacon is crispy. While first batch cooks, wrap the remaining livers. Repeat step 6 to cook your second batch.

Goat Cheese and Garlic Crostini

Prep time: 3 minutes | Cook time: 5 minutes | Serves 4

1 wholemeal baguette
60 ml olive oil
2 garlic cloves, minced

113 g goat cheese
2 tablespoons fresh basil, minced

Preheat the air fryer to 190ºC. Cut the baguette into ½-inch-thick slices. In a small bowl, mix together the olive oil and garlic, then brush it over one side of each slice of bread. Place the olive-oil-coated bread in a single layer in the air fryer basket and bake for 5 minutes. Meanwhile, in a small bowl, mix together the goat cheese and basil. Remove the toast from the air fryer, then spread a thin layer of the goat cheese mixture over the top of each piece and serve.

Cheesy Hash Brown Bruschetta

Prep time: 5 minutes | Cook time: 6 to 8 minutes | Serves 4

4 frozen hash brown patties
1 tablespoon olive oil
80 ml chopped cherry tomatoes
3 tablespoons diced fresh Mozzarella

2 tablespoons grated Parmesan cheese
1 tablespoon balsamic vinegar
1 tablespoon minced fresh basil

4 frozen hash brown patties 1 tablespoon olive oil 80 ml chopped cherry tomatoes 3 tablespoons diced fresh Mozzarella 2 tablespoons grated Parmesan cheese 1 tablespoon balsamic vinegar 1 tablespoon minced fresh basil

Parmesan French Fries

Prep time: 10 minutes | Cook time: 15 minutes per batch | Serves 2

2 to 3 large russet or Maris Piper potatoes, peeled and cut into ½-inch sticks
2 teaspoons vegetable or rapeseed oil
177 ml grated Parmesan cheese

½ teaspoon salt
Freshly ground black pepper, to taste
1 teaspoon fresh chopped parsley

Bring a large saucepan of salted water to a boil on the stovetop while you peel and cut the potatoes. Blanch the potatoes in the boiling salted water for 4 minutes while you preheat the air fryer to 200ºC. Strain the potatoes and rinse them with cold water. Dry them well with a clean kitchen towel. Toss the dried potato sticks gently with the oil and place them in the air fryer basket. Air fry for 25 minutes, shaking the basket a few times while the fries cook to help them brown evenly. Combine the Parmesan cheese, salt and pepper. With 2 minutes left on the air fryer cooking time, sprinkle the fries with the Parmesan cheese mixture. Toss the fries to coat them evenly with the cheese mixture and continue to air fry for the final 2 minutes, until the cheese has melted and just starts to brown. Sprinkle the finished fries with chopped parsley, a little more grated Parmesan cheese if you like, and serve.

Vegetable Pot Stickers

Prep time: 12 minutes | Cook time: 11 to 18 minutes | Makes 12 pot stickers

240 ml shredded red cabbage
60 ml chopped button mushrooms
60 ml grated carrot
2 tablespoons minced onion

2 garlic cloves, minced
2 teaspoons grated fresh ginger
12 gyoza/pot sticker wrappers
2½ teaspoons olive oil, divided

In a baking pan, combine the red cabbage, mushrooms, carrot, onion, garlic, and ginger. Add 1 tablespoon of water. Place in the air fryer and air fry at 190ºC for 3 to 6 minutes, until the vegetables are crisp-tender. Drain and set aside. Working one at a time, place the pot sticker wrappers on a work surface. Top each wrapper with a scant 1 tablespoon of the filling. Fold half of the wrapper over the other half to form a half circle. Dab one edge with water and press both edges together. To another pan, add 1¼ teaspoons of olive oil. Put half of the pot stickers, seam-side up, in the pan. Air fry for 5 minutes, or until the bottoms are light golden brown. Add 1 tablespoon of water and return the pan to the air fryer. Air fry for 4 to 6 minutes more, or until hot. Repeat with the remaining pot stickers, remaining 1¼ teaspoons of oil, and another tablespoon of water. Serve immediately.

Sea Salt Potato Crisps

Prep time: 30 minutes | Cook time: 27 minutes | Serves 4

Oil, for spraying
4 medium yellow potatoes such
as Maris Pipers

1 tablespoon oil
⅛ to ¼ teaspoon fine sea salt

Line the air fryer basket with parchment and spray lightly with oil. Using a mandoline or a very sharp knife, cut the potatoes into very thin slices. Place the slices in a bowl of cold water and let soak for about 20 minutes. Drain the potatoes, transfer them to a plate lined with paper towels, and pat dry. Drizzle the oil over the potatoes, sprinkle with the salt, and toss to combine. Transfer to the prepared basket. Air fry at 90ºC for 20 minutes. Toss the crisps, increase the heat to 200ºC, and cook for another 5 to 7 minutes, until crispy.

Feta and Quinoa Stuffed Mushrooms

Prep time: 5 minutes | Cook time: 8 minutes | Serves 6

2 tablespoons finely diced red
pepper
1 garlic clove, minced
60 ml cooked quinoa
⅛ teaspoon salt
¼ teaspoon dried oregano

24 button mushrooms, stemmed
57 g crumbled feta
3 tablespoons wholemeal
breadcrumbs
Olive oil cooking spray

Preheat the air fryer to 180ºC. In a small bowl, combine the pepper, garlic, quinoa, salt, and oregano. Spoon the quinoa stuffing into the mushroom caps until just filled. Add a small piece of feta to the top of each mushroom. Sprinkle a pinch breadcrumbs over the feta on each mushroom. Spray the basket of the air fryer with olive oil cooking spray, then gently place the mushrooms into the basket, making sure that they don't touch each other. (Depending on the size of the air fryer, you may have to cook them in two batches.) Place the basket into the air fryer and bake for 8 minutes. Remove from the air fryer and serve.

Shrimp Pirogues

Prep time: 15 minutes | Cook time: 4 to 5 minutes |
Serves 8

340 g small, peeled, and
deveined raw shrimp
85 g soft white cheese, room
temperature
2 tablespoons natural yoghurt
1 teaspoon lemon juice

1 teaspoon dried dill weed,
crushed
Salt, to taste
4 small hothouse cucumbers,
each approximately 6 inches
long

Pour 4 tablespoons water in bottom of air fryer drawer. Place shrimp in air fryer basket in single layer and air fry at 200ºC for 4 to 5 minutes, just until done. Watch carefully because shrimp cooks quickly, and overcooking makes it tough. Chop shrimp into small pieces, no larger than ½ inch. Refrigerate while mixing the remaining ingredients. With a fork, mash and whip the soft white cheese until smooth. Stir in the yoghurt and beat until smooth. Stir in lemon juice, dill weed, and chopped shrimp. Taste for seasoning. If needed, add ¼ to ½ teaspoon salt to suit your taste. Store in refrigerator until serving time. When ready to serve, wash and dry cucumbers and split them lengthwise. Scoop out the seeds and turn cucumbers upside down on paper towels to drain for 10 minutes. Just before filling, wipe centres of cucumbers dry. Spoon the shrimp mixture into the pirogues and cut in half crosswise. Serve immediately.

Bacon-Wrapped Shrimp and Jalapeño

Prep time: 20 minutes | Cook time: 26 minutes | Serves 8

24 large shrimp, peeled and
deveined, about 340 g
5 tablespoons barbecue sauce,

divided
12 strips bacon, cut in half
24 small pickled jalapeño slices

Toss together the shrimp and 3 tablespoons of the barbecue sauce. Let stand for 15 minutes. Soak 24 wooden toothpicks in water for 10 minutes. Wrap 1 piece bacon around the shrimp and jalapeño slice, then secure with a toothpick. Preheat the air fryer to 175ºC. Working in batches, place half of the shrimp in the air fryer basket, spacing them ½ inch apart. Air fry for 10 minutes. Turn shrimp over with tongs and air fry for 3 minutes more, or until bacon is golden brown and shrimp are cooked through. Brush with the remaining barbecue sauce and serve.

Grilled Ham and Cheese on Raisin Bread

Prep time: 5 minutes | Cook time: 10 minutes | Serves 1

2 slices raisin bread or fruit loaf
2 tablespoons butter, softened
2 teaspoons honey mustard
3 slices thinly sliced honey

roast ham (about 85 g)
4 slices Muenster cheese (about
85 g)
2 toothpicks

Preheat the air fryer to 190ºC. Spread the softened butter on one side of both slices of bread and place the bread, buttered side down on the counter. Spread the honey mustard on the other side of each slice of bread. Layer 2 slices of cheese, the ham and the remaining 2 slices of cheese on one slice of bread and top with the other slice of bread. Remember to leave the buttered side of the bread on the outside. Transfer the sandwich to the air fryer basket and secure the sandwich with toothpicks. Air fry for 5 minutes. Flip the sandwich over, remove the toothpicks and air fry for another 5 minutes. Cut the sandwich in half and enjoy!

Stuffed Figs with Goat Cheese and Honey

Prep time: 5 minutes | Cook time: 10 minutes | Serves 4

8 fresh figs	1 tablespoon honey, plus more
57 g goat cheese	for serving
¼ teaspoon ground cinnamon	1 tablespoon olive oil

Preheat the air fryer to 180ºC. Line an 8-by-8-inch baking dish with parchment paper that comes up the side so you can lift it out after cooking. In a large bowl, mix together all of the ingredients until well combined. Press the oat mixture into the pan in an even layer. Place the pan into the air fryer basket and bake for 15 minutes. Remove the pan from the air fryer and lift the granola cake out of the pan using the edges of the parchment paper. Allow to cool for 5 minutes before slicing into 6 equal bars. Serve immediately or wrap in plastic wrap and store at room temperature for up to 1 week.

Shishito Peppers with Herb Dressing

Prep time: 10 minutes | Cook time: 6 minutes | Serves 2 to 4

170 g shishito or Padron peppers	fresh flat-leaf parsley
1 tablespoon vegetable oil	1 tablespoon finely chopped fresh tarragon
Rock salt and freshly ground black pepper, to taste	1 tablespoon finely chopped fresh chives
120 ml mayonnaise	Finely grated zest of ½ lemon
2 tablespoons finely chopped fresh basil leaves	1 tablespoon fresh lemon juice
2 tablespoons finely chopped	Flaky sea salt, for serving

Preheat the air fryer to 200ºC. In a bowl, toss together the shishitos and oil to evenly coat and season with rock salt and black pepper. Transfer to the air fryer and air fry for 6 minutes, shaking the basket halfway through, or until the shishitos are blistered and lightly charred. Meanwhile, in a small bowl, whisk together the mayonnaise, basil, parsley, tarragon, chives, lemon zest, and lemon juice. Pile the peppers on a plate, sprinkle with flaky sea salt, and serve hot with the dressing.

Garlic-Parmesan Croutons

Prep time: 3 minutes | Cook time: 12 minutes | Serves 4

Oil, for spraying	3 tablespoons olive oil
1 L cubed French bread	1 tablespoon granulated garlic
1 tablespoon grated Parmesan cheese	½ teaspoon unsalted salt

Line the air fryer basket with parchment and spray lightly with oil. In a large bowl, mix together the bread, Parmesan cheese, olive oil, garlic, and salt, tossing with your hands to evenly distribute the seasonings. Transfer the coated bread cubes to the prepared basket. Air fry at 175ºC for 10 to 12 minutes, stirring once after 5 minutes, or until crisp and golden brown.

Caramelized Onion Dip with White Cheese

Prep time: 5 minutes | Cook time: 30 minutes | Serves 8 to 10

1 tablespoon butter	¼ teaspoon onion powder
1 medium onion, halved and thinly sliced	1 tablespoon chopped fresh chives
¼ teaspoon rock salt, plus additional for seasoning	Black pepper, to taste
113 g soft white cheese	Thick-cut potato crisps or vegetable crisps
120 ml sour cream	

Place the butter in a baking pan. Place the pan in the air fryer basket. Set the air fryer to 90ºC for 1 minute, or until the butter is melted. Add the onions and salt to the pan. Set the air fryer to 90ºC for 15 minutes, or until onions are softened. Set the air fryer to 190ºC for 15 minutes, until onions are a deep golden brown, stirring two or three times during the cooking time. Let cool completely. In a medium bowl, stir together the cooked onions, soft white cheese, sour cream, onion powder, and chives. Season with salt and pepper. Cover and refrigerate for 2 hours to allow the flavours to blend. Serve the dip with potato crisps or vegetable crisps.

Soft white cheese Stuffed Jalapeño Poppers

Prep time: 12 minutes | Cook time: 6 to 8 minutes | Serves 10

227 g soft white cheese, at room temperature	minced
240 ml panko breadcrumbs, divided	1 teaspoon chilli powder
2 tablespoons fresh parsley,	10 jalapeño peppers, halved and seeded
	Cooking oil spray

In a small bowl, whisk the soft white cheese, 120 ml of panko, the parsley, and chilli powder until combined. Stuff the cheese mixture into the jalapeño halves. Sprinkle the tops of the stuffed jalapeños with the remaining 120 ml of panko and press it lightly into the filling. Insert the crisper plate into the basket and the basket into the unit. Preheat the unit by selecting AIR FRY, setting the temperature to 190ºC, and setting the time to 3 minutes. Select START/STOP to begin. Once the unit is preheated, spray the crisper plate with cooking oil. Place the poppers into the basket. Select AIR FRY, set the temperature to 190ºC, and set the time to 8 minutes. Select START/STOP to begin. After 6 minutes, check the poppers. If they are softened and the cheese is melted, they are done. If not, resume cooking. When the cooking is complete, serve warm.

Greek Potato Skins with Olives and Feta

Prep time: 5 minutes | Cook time: 45 minutes | Serves 4

2 russet or Maris Piper potatoes

3 tablespoons olive oil, divided, plus more for drizzling (optional)

1 teaspoon rock salt, divided

¼ teaspoon black pepper

2 tablespoons fresh coriander, chopped, plus more for serving

60 ml Kalamata olives, diced

60 ml crumbled feta

Chopped fresh parsley, for garnish (optional)

Preheat the air fryer to 190°C. Using a fork, poke 2 to 3 holes in the potatoes, then coat each with about ½ tablespoon olive oil and ½ teaspoon salt. Place the potatoes into the air fryer basket and bake for 30 minutes. Remove the potatoes from the air fryer, and slice in half. Using a spoon, scoop out the flesh of the potatoes, leaving a ½-inch layer of potato inside the skins, and set the skins aside. In a medium bowl, combine the scooped potato middles with the remaining 2 tablespoons of olive oil, ½ teaspoon of salt, black pepper, and coriander. Mix until well combined. Divide the potato filling into the now-empty potato skins, spreading it evenly over them. Top each potato with a tablespoon each of the olives and feta. Place the loaded potato skins back into the air fryer and bake for 15 minutes. Serve with additional chopped coriander or parsley and a drizzle of olive oil, if desired.

Crispy Breaded Beef Cubes

Prep time: 10 minutes | Cook time: 12 to 16 minutes | Serves 4

450 g sirloin tip, cut into 1-inch cubes

240 ml cheese pasta sauce

355 ml soft breadcrumbs

2 tablespoons olive oil

½ teaspoon dried marjoram

Preheat the air fryer to 180°C. In a medium bowl, toss the beef with the pasta sauce to coat. In a shallow bowl, combine the breadcrumbs, oil, and marjoram, and mix well. Drop the beef cubes, one at a time, into the bread crumb mixture to coat thoroughly. Air fry the beef in two batches for 6 to 8 minutes, shaking the basket once during cooking time, until the beef is at least 60°C and the outside is crisp and brown. Serve hot.

Garlic-Roasted Tomatoes and Olives

Prep time: 5 minutes | Cook time: 20 minutes | Serves 6

475 ml cherry tomatoes

4 garlic cloves, roughly chopped

½ red onion, roughly chopped

240 ml black olives

240 ml green olives

1 tablespoon fresh basil, minced

1 tablespoon fresh oregano, minced

2 tablespoons olive oil

¼ to ½ teaspoon salt

Preheat the air fryer to 190°C. In a large bowl, combine all of the ingredients and toss together so that the tomatoes and olives are coated well with the olive oil and herbs. Pour the mixture into the air fryer basket, and roast for 10 minutes. Stir the mixture well, then continue roasting for an additional 10 minutes. Remove from the air fryer, transfer to a serving bowl, and enjoy.

Chapter 5 Vegetables and Sides

Burger Bun for One

Prep time: 2 minutes | Cook time: 5 minutes | Serves 1

2 tablespoons salted butter, melted

25 g blanched finely ground almond flour

¼ teaspoon baking powder

⅛ teaspoon apple cider vinegar

1 large egg, whisked

Pour butter into an ungreased ramekin. Add flour, baking powder, and vinegar to ramekin and stir until combined. Add egg and stir until batter is mostly smooth. Place ramekin into air fryer basket. Adjust the temperature to 180°C and bake for 5 minutes. When done, the centre will be firm and the top slightly browned. Let cool, about 5 minutes, then remove from ramekin and slice in half. Serve.

Citrus-Roasted Broccoli Florets

Prep time: 5 minutes | Cook time: 12 minutes | Serves 6

285 g broccoli florets (approximately 1 large head)

2 tablespoons olive oil

½ teaspoon salt

130 ml orange juice

1 tablespoon raw honey

Orange wedges, for serving (optional)

Preheat the air fryer to 180°C. In a large bowl, combine the broccoli, olive oil, salt, orange juice, and honey. Toss the broccoli in the liquid until well coated. Pour the broccoli mixture into the air fryer basket and roast for 6 minutes. Stir and roast for 6 minutes more. Serve alone or with orange wedges for additional citrus flavour, if desired.

Gold Artichoke Hearts

Prep time: 15 minutes | Cook time: 8 minutes | Serves 4

12 whole artichoke hearts packed in water, drained

60 g plain flour

1 egg

40 g panko bread crumbs

1 teaspoon Italian seasoning

Cooking oil spray

Squeeze any excess water from the artichoke hearts and place them on paper towels to dry. Place the flour in a small bowl. In another small bowl, beat the egg. In a third small bowl, stir together the panko and Italian seasoning. Dip the artichoke hearts in the flour, in the egg, and into the panko mixture until coated. Insert the crisper plate into the basket and the basket into the unit. Preheat the unit by selecting AIR FRY, setting the temperature to 190°C, and setting the time to 3 minutes. Select START/STOP to begin. Once the unit is preheated, spray the crisper plate and the basket with cooking oil. Place the breaded artichoke hearts into the basket, stacking them if needed. Select AIR FRY, set the temperature to 190°C, and set the time to 8 minutes. Select START/STOP to begin. After 4 minutes, use tongs to flip the artichoke hearts. I recommend flipping instead of shaking because the hearts are small, and this will help keep the breading intact. Re-insert the basket to resume cooking. 1When the cooking is complete, the artichoke hearts should be deep golden brown and crisp. Cool for 5 minutes before serving.

Easy Rosemary Green Beans

Prep time: 5 minutes | Cook time: 5 minutes | Serves 1

1 tablespoon butter, melted

2 tablespoons rosemary

½ teaspoon salt

3 cloves garlic, minced

95 g chopped green beans

Preheat the air fryer to 200°C. Combine the melted butter with the rosemary, salt, and minced garlic. Toss in the green beans, coating them well. Air fry for 5 minutes. Serve immediately.

Courgette Fritters

Prep time: 10 minutes | Cook time: 10 minutes | Serves 4

2 courgette, grated (about 450 g)

1 teaspoon salt

25 g almond flour

20 g grated Parmesan cheese

1 large egg

¼ teaspoon dried thyme

¼ teaspoon ground turmeric

¼ teaspoon freshly ground black pepper

1 tablespoon olive oil

½ lemon, sliced into wedges

Preheat the air fryer to 200°C. Cut a piece of parchment paper to fit slightly smaller than the bottom of the air fryer. Place the courgette in a large colander and sprinkle with the salt. Let sit for 5 to 10 minutes. Squeeze as much liquid as you can from the courgette and place in a large mixing bowl. Add the almond flour, Parmesan, egg, thyme, turmeric, and black pepper. Stir gently until thoroughly combined. Shape the mixture into 8 patties and arrange on the parchment paper. Brush lightly with the olive oil. Pausing halfway through the cooking time to turn the patties, air fry for 10 minutes until golden brown. Serve warm with the lemon wedges.

Sesame Taj Tofu

Prep time: 5 minutes | Cook time: 25 minutes | Serves 4

1 block firm tofu, pressed and
cut into 1-inch thick cubes
2 tablespoons soy sauce
2 teaspoons toasted sesame

seeds
1 teaspoon rice vinegar
1 tablespoon cornflour

Preheat the air fryer to 200ºC. Add the tofu, soy sauce, sesame seeds, and rice vinegar in a bowl together and mix well to coat the tofu cubes. Then cover the tofu in cornflour and put it in the air fryer basket. Air fry for 25 minutes, giving the basket a shake at five-minute intervals to ensure the tofu cooks evenly. Serve immediately.

Garlic-Parmesan Crispy Baby Potatoes

Prep time: 10 minutes | Cook time: 15 minutes | Serves 4

Oil, for spraying
450 g baby potatoes
45 g grated Parmesan cheese,
divided
3 tablespoons olive oil
2 teaspoons garlic powder
½ teaspoon onion powder

½ teaspoon salt
¼ teaspoon freshly ground
black pepper
¼ teaspoon paprika
2 tablespoons chopped fresh
parsley, for garnish

Line the air fryer basket with parchment and spray lightly with oil. Rinse the potatoes, pat dry with paper towels, and place in a large bowl. In a small bowl, mix together 45 g of Parmesan cheese, the olive oil, garlic, onion powder, salt, black pepper, and paprika. Pour the mixture over the potatoes and toss to coat. Transfer the potatoes to the prepared basket and spread them out in an even layer, taking care to keep them from touching. You may need to work in batches, depending on the size of your air fryer. Air fry at 200ºC for 15 minutes, stirring after 7 to 8 minutes, or until easily pierced with a fork. Continue to cook for another 1 to 2 minutes, if needed. Sprinkle with the parsley and the remaining Parmesan cheese and serve.

Bacon-Wrapped Asparagus

Prep time: 10 minutes | Cook time: 10 minutes | Serves 4

8 slices reduced-sodium bacon, cut in half
16 thick (about 450 g) asparagus spears, trimmed of woody ends

Preheat the air fryer to 180ºC. Wrap a half piece of bacon around the centre of each stalk of asparagus. Working in batches, if necessary, arrange seam-side down in a single layer in the air fryer basket. Air fry for 10 minutes until the bacon is crisp and the stalks are tender.

Buttery Mushrooms

Prep time: 10 minutes | Cook time: 10 minutes | Serves 4

230 g shitake mushrooms,
halved
2 tablespoons salted butter,
melted

¼ teaspoon salt
¼ teaspoon ground black
pepper

In a medium bowl, toss mushrooms with butter, then sprinkle with salt and pepper. Place into ungreased air fryer basket. Adjust the temperature to 200ºC and air fry for 10 minutes, shaking the basket halfway through cooking. Mushrooms will be tender when done. Serve warm.

Ricotta Potatoes

Prep time: 15 minutes | Cook time: 15 minutes | Serves 4

4 potatoes
2 tablespoons olive oil
110 g Ricotta cheese, at room
temperature
2 tablespoons chopped spring
onions
1 tablespoon roughly chopped

fresh parsley
1 tablespoon minced coriander
60 g Cheddar cheese, preferably
freshly grated
1 teaspoon celery seeds
½ teaspoon salt
½ teaspoon garlic pepper

Preheat the air fryer to 180ºC. Pierce the skin of the potatoes with a knife. Air fry in the air fryer basket for 13 minutes. If they are not cooked through by this time, leave for 2 to 3 minutes longer. In the meantime, make the stuffing by combining all the other ingredients. Cut halfway into the cooked potatoes to open them. Spoon equal amounts of the stuffing into each potato and serve hot.

Fig, Chickpea, and Rocket Salad

Prep time: 15 minutes | Cook time: 20 minutes | Serves 4

8 fresh figs, halved
250 g cooked chickpeas
1 teaspoon crushed roasted
cumin seeds
4 tablespoons balsamic vinegar

2 tablespoons extra-virgin olive
oil, plus more for greasing
Salt and ground black pepper,
to taste
40 g rocket, washed and dried

Preheat the air fryer to 190ºC. Cover the air fryer basket with aluminum foil and grease lightly with oil. Put the figs in the air fryer basket and air fry for 10 minutes. In a bowl, combine the chickpeas and cumin seeds. Remove the air fried figs from the air fryer and replace with the chickpeas. Air fry for 10 minutes. Leave to cool. In the meantime, prepare the dressing. Mix the balsamic vinegar, olive oil, salt and pepper. In a salad bowl, combine the rocket with the cooled figs and chickpeas. Toss with the sauce and serve.

Curried Fruit

Prep time: 10 minutes | Cook time: 20 minutes |
Serves 6 to 8

210 g cubed fresh pineapple	425 g can dark, sweet, pitted
200 g cubed fresh pear (firm,	cherries with juice
not overly ripe)	2 tablespoons brown sugar
230 g frozen peaches, thawed	1 teaspoon curry powder

Combine all ingredients in large bowl. Stir gently to mix in the sugar and curry. Pour into a baking pan and bake at 180°C for 10 minutes. Stir fruit and cook 10 more minutes. Serve hot.

Shishito Pepper Roast

Prep time: 4 minutes | Cook time: 9 minutes | Serves 4

Cooking oil spray (sunflower,	1 tablespoon soy sauce
safflower, or refined coconut)	2 teaspoons freshly squeezed
450 g shishito, Anaheim, or bell	lime juice
peppers, rinsed	2 large garlic cloves, pressed

Insert the crisper plate into the basket and the basket into the unit. Preheat the unit by selecting AIR ROAST, setting the temperature to 200°C, and setting the time to 3 minutes. Select START/STOP to begin. Once the unit is preheated, spray the crisper plate and the basket with cooking oil. Place the peppers into the basket and spray them with oil. Select AIR ROAST, set the temperature to 200°C, and set the time to 9 minutes. Select START/STOP to begin. After 3 minutes, remove the basket and shake the peppers. Spray the peppers with more oil. Reinsert the basket to resume cooking. Repeat this step again after 3 minutes. While the peppers roast, in a medium bowl, whisk the soy sauce, lime juice, and garlic until combined. Set aside. When the cooking is complete, several of the peppers should have lots of nice browned spots on them. If using Anaheim or bell peppers, cut a slit in the side of each pepper and remove the seeds, which can be bitter. Place the roasted peppers in the bowl with the sauce. Toss to coat the peppers evenly and serve.

Crispy Green Beans

Prep time: 5 minutes | Cook time: 8 minutes | Serves 4

2 teaspoons olive oil	¼ teaspoon salt
230 g fresh green beans, ends	¼ teaspoon ground black
trimmed	pepper

In a large bowl, drizzle olive oil over green beans and sprinkle with salt and pepper. Place green beans into ungreased air fryer basket. Adjust the temperature to 180°C and set the timer for 8 minutes, shaking the basket two times during cooking. Green beans will be dark golden and crispy at the edges when done. Serve warm.

Parsnip Fries with Romesco Sauce

Prep time: 20 minutes | Cook time: 24 minutes | Serves 4

Romesco Sauce:	seeded
1 red pepper, halved and seeded	1 tablespoon red wine vinegar
1 (1-inch) thick slice of Italian	¼ teaspoon smoked paprika
bread, torn into pieces	½ teaspoon salt
130 g almonds, toasted	180 ml olive oil
Olive oil	3 parsnips, peeled and cut into
½ Jalapeño pepper, seeded	long strips
1 tablespoon fresh parsley	2 teaspoons olive oil
leaves	Salt and freshly ground black
1 clove garlic	pepper, to taste
2 plum tomatoes, peeled and	

Preheat the air fryer to 200°C. Place the red pepper halves, cut side down, in the air fryer basket and air fry for 8 to 10 minutes, or until the skin turns black all over. Remove the pepper from the air fryer and let it cool. When it is cool enough to handle, peel the pepper. Toss the torn bread and almonds with a little olive oil and air fry for 4 minutes, shaking the basket a couple times throughout the cooking time. When the bread and almonds are nicely toasted, remove them from the air fryer and let them cool for just a minute or two. Combine the toasted bread, almonds, roasted red pepper, Jalapeño pepper, parsley, garlic, tomatoes, vinegar, smoked paprika and salt in a food processor or blender. Process until smooth. With the processor running, add the olive oil through the feed tube until the sauce comes together in a smooth paste that is barely pourable. Toss the parsnip strips with the olive oil, salt and freshly ground black pepper and air fry at 200°C for 10 minutes, shaking the basket a couple times during the cooking process so they brown and cook evenly. Serve the parsnip fries warm with the Romesco sauce to dip into.

Hawaiian Brown Rice

Prep time: 10 minutes | Cook time: 12 to 16 minutes
| Serves 4 to 6

110 g ground sausage	380 g cooked brown rice
1 teaspoon butter	1 (230 g) can crushed
20 g minced onion	pineapple, drained
40 g minced bell pepper	

Shape sausage into 3 or 4 thin patties. Air fry at 200°C for 6 to 8 minutes or until well done. Remove from air fryer, drain, and crumble. Set aside. Place butter, onion, and bell pepper in baking pan. Roast at 200°C for 1 minute and stir. Cook 3 to 4 minutes longer or just until vegetables are tender. Add sausage, rice, and pineapple to vegetables and stir together. Roast for 2 to 3 minutes, until heated through.

Green Peas with Mint

Prep time: 5 minutes | Cook time: 5 minutes | Serves 4

75 g shredded lettuce

1 (280 g) package frozen green peas, thawed

1 tablespoon fresh mint, shredded

1 teaspoon melted butter

Lay the shredded lettuce in the air fryer basket. Toss together the peas, mint, and melted butter and spoon over the lettuce. Air fry at 180°C for 5 minutes, until peas are warm and lettuce wilts.

Butter and Garlic Fried Cabbage

Prep time: 5 minutes | Cook time: 9 minutes | Serves 2

Oil, for spraying

½ head cabbage, cut into bite-size pieces

2 tablespoons unsalted butter, melted

1 teaspoon granulated garlic

½ teaspoon coarse sea salt

¼ teaspoon freshly ground black pepper

Line the air fryer basket with parchment and spray lightly with oil. In a large bowl, mix together the cabbage, butter, garlic, salt, and black pepper until evenly coated. Transfer the cabbage to the prepared basket and spray lightly with oil. Air fry at 190°C for 5 minutes, toss, and cook for another 3 to 4 minutes, or until lightly crispy.

Chiles Rellenos with Red Chile Sauce

Prep time: 20 minutes | Cook time: 20 minutes | Serves 2

Peppers:

2 poblano peppers, rinsed and dried

110 g thawed frozen or drained canned corn kernels

1 spring onion, sliced

2 tablespoons chopped fresh coriander

½ teaspoon coarse sea salt

¼ teaspoon black pepper

150 g grated Monterey Jack cheese

Sauce:

3 tablespoons extra-virgin olive

oil

25 g finely chopped yellow onion

2 teaspoons minced garlic

1 (170 g) can tomato paste

2 tablespoons ancho chili powder

1 teaspoon dried oregano

1 teaspoon ground cumin

½ teaspoon coarse sea salt

470 ml chicken stock

2 tablespoons fresh lemon juice

Mexican crema or sour cream, for serving

For the peppers: Place the peppers in the air fryer basket. Set the air fryer to 200°C for 10 minutes, turning the peppers halfway through the cooking time, until their skins are charred. Transfer the peppers to a resealable plastic bag, seal, and set aside to steam for 5 minutes. Peel the peppers and discard the skins. Cut a slit down the centre of each pepper, starting at the stem and continuing to the tip. Remove the seeds, being careful not to tear the chile. In a medium bowl, combine the corn, spring onion, coriander, salt, black pepper, and cheese; set aside. Meanwhile, for the sauce: In a large skillet, heat the olive oil over medium-high heat. Add the onion and cook, stirring, until tender, about 5 minutes. Add the garlic and cook, stirring, for 30 seconds. Stir in the tomato paste, chile powder, oregano, and cumin, and salt. Cook, stirring, for 1 minute. Whisk in the stock and lemon juice. Bring to a simmer and cook, stirring occasionally, while the stuffed peppers finish cooking. Cut a slit down the centre of each poblano pepper, starting at the stem and continuing to the tip. Remove the seeds, being careful not to tear the chile. Carefully stuff each pepper with half the corn mixture. Place the stuffed peppers in a baking pan. Place the pan in the air fryer basket. Set the air fryer to 200°C for 10 minutes, or until the cheese has melted. Transfer the stuffed peppers to a serving platter and drizzle with the sauce and some crema.

Courgette Balls

Prep time: 5 minutes | Cook time: 10 minutes | Serves 4

4 courgettes

1 egg

45 g grated Parmesan cheese

1 tablespoon Italian herbs

75 g grated coconut

Thinly grate the courgettes and dry with a cheesecloth, ensuring to remove all the moisture. In a bowl, combine the courgettes with the egg, Parmesan, Italian herbs, and grated coconut, mixing well to incorporate everything. Using the hands, mold the mixture into balls. Preheat the air fryer to 200°C. Lay the courgette balls in the air fryer basket and air fry for 10 minutes. Serve hot.

Garlic Parmesan-Roasted Cauliflower

Prep time: 5 minutes | Cook time: 15 minutes | Serves 6

1 medium head cauliflower, leaves and core removed, cut into florets

2 tablespoons salted butter, melted

½ tablespoon salt

2 cloves garlic, peeled and finely minced

45 g grated Parmesan cheese, divided

Toss cauliflower in a large bowl with butter. Sprinkle with salt, garlic, and ½ of the Parmesan. Place florets into ungreased air fryer basket. Adjust the temperature to 180°C and roast for 15 minutes, shaking basket halfway through cooking. Cauliflower will be browned at the edges and tender when done. Transfer florets to a large serving dish and sprinkle with remaining Parmesan. Serve warm.

Sweet and Crispy Roasted Pearl Onions

Prep time: 5 minutes | Cook time: 18 minutes | Serves 3

1 (410 g) package frozen pearl onions (do not thaw)
2 tablespoons extra-virgin olive oil
2 tablespoons balsamic vinegar
2 teaspoons finely chopped fresh rosemary
½ teaspoon coarse sea salt
¼ teaspoon black pepper

In a medium bowl, combine the onions, olive oil, vinegar, rosemary, salt, and pepper until well coated. Transfer the onions to the air fryer basket. Set the air fryer to 200°C for 18 minutes, or until the onions are tender and lightly charred, stirring once or twice during the cooking time.

Mushrooms with Goat Cheese

Prep time: 10 minutes | Cook time: 10 minutes | Serves 4

3 tablespoons vegetable oil
450 g mixed mushrooms, trimmed and sliced
1 clove garlic, minced
¼ teaspoon dried thyme
½ teaspoon black pepper
110 g goat cheese, diced
2 teaspoons chopped fresh thyme leaves (optional)

In a baking pan, combine the oil, mushrooms, garlic, dried thyme, and pepper. Stir in the goat cheese. Place the pan in the air fryer basket. Set the air fryer to 200°C for 10 minutes, stirring halfway through the cooking time. Sprinkle with fresh thyme, if desired.

Mashed Sweet Potato Tots

Prep time: 10 minutes | Cook time: 12 to 13 minutes per batch | Makes 18 to 24 tots

210 g cooked mashed sweet potatoes
1 egg white, beaten
⅛ teaspoon ground cinnamon
1 dash nutmeg
2 tablespoons chopped pecans
1½ teaspoons honey
Salt, to taste
50 g panko bread crumbs
Oil for misting or cooking spray

Preheat the air fryer to 200°C. In a large bowl, mix together the potatoes, egg white, cinnamon, nutmeg, pecans, honey, and salt to taste. Place panko crumbs on a sheet of wax paper. For each tot, use about 2 teaspoons of sweet potato mixture. To shape, drop the measure of potato mixture onto panko crumbs and push crumbs up and around potatoes to coat edges. Then turn tot over to coat other side with crumbs. Mist tots with oil or cooking spray and place in air fryer basket in single layer. Air fry at 200°C for 12 to 13 minutes, until browned and crispy. Repeat steps 5 and 6 to cook remaining tots.

Parmesan Herb Focaccia Bread

Prep time: 10 minutes | Cook time: 10 minutes | Serves 6

225 g shredded Mozzarella cheese
30 g) full-fat cream cheese
95 g blanched finely ground almond flour
40 g ground golden flaxseed
20 g grated Parmesan cheese
½ teaspoon bicarbonate of soda
2 large eggs
½ teaspoon garlic powder
¼ teaspoon dried basil
¼ teaspoon dried rosemary
2 tablespoons salted butter, melted and divided

Place Mozzarella, cream cheese, and almond flour into a large microwave-safe bowl and microwave for 1 minute. Add the flaxseed, Parmesan, and bicarbonate of soda and stir until smooth ball forms. If the mixture cools too much, it will be hard to mix. Return to microwave for 10 to 15 seconds to rewarm if necessary. Stir in eggs. You may need to use your hands to get them fully incorporated. Just keep stirring and they will absorb into the dough. Sprinkle dough with garlic powder, basil, and rosemary and knead into dough. Grease a baking pan with 1 tablespoon melted butter. Press the dough evenly into the pan. Place pan into the air fryer basket. Adjust the temperature to 200°C and bake for 10 minutes. At 7 minutes, cover with foil if bread begins to get too dark. Remove and let cool at least 30 minutes. Drizzle with remaining butter and serve.

Cabbage Wedges with Caraway Butter

Prep time: 30 minutes | Cook time: 35 to 40 minutes | Serves 6

1 tablespoon caraway seeds
110 g unsalted butter, at room temperature
½ teaspoon grated lemon zest
1 small head green or red
cabbage, cut into 6 wedges
1 tablespoon avocado oil
½ teaspoon sea salt
¼ teaspoon freshly ground black pepper

Place the caraway seeds in a small dry skillet over medium-high heat. Toast the seeds for 2 to 3 minutes, then remove them from the heat and let cool. Lightly crush the seeds using a mortar and pestle or with the back of a knife. Place the butter in a small bowl and stir in the crushed caraway seeds and lemon zest. Form the butter into a log and wrap it in parchment paper or plastic wrap. Refrigerate for at least 1 hour or freeze for 20 minutes. Brush or spray the cabbage wedges with the avocado oil, and sprinkle with the salt and pepper. Set the air fryer to190°C. Place the cabbage in a single layer in the air fryer basket and roast for 20 minutes. Flip and cook for 15 to 20 minutes more, until the cabbage is tender and lightly charred. Plate the cabbage and dot with caraway butter. Tent with foil for 5 minutes to melt the butter, and serve.

Lebanese Baba Ghanoush

Prep time: 15 minutes | Cook time: 20 minutes | Serves 4

1 medium aubergine	1 tablespoon extra-virgin olive
2 tablespoons vegetable oil	oil
2 tablespoons tahini (sesame	½ teaspoon smoked paprika
paste)	2 tablespoons chopped fresh
2 tablespoons fresh lemon juice	parsley
½ teaspoon coarse sea salt	

Rub the aubergine all over with the vegetable oil. Place the aubergine in the air fryer basket. Set the air fryer to 200ºC for 20 minutes, or until the aubergine skin is blistered and charred. Transfer the aubergine to a re-sealable plastic bag, seal, and set aside for 15 minutes (the aubergine will finish cooking in the residual heat trapped in the bag). Transfer the aubergine to a large bowl. Peel off and discard the charred skin. Roughly mash the aubergine flesh. Add the tahini, lemon juice, and salt. Stir to combine. Transfer the mixture to a serving bowl. Drizzle with the olive oil. Sprinkle with the paprika and parsley and serve.

Glazed Carrots

Prep time: 10 minutes | Cook time: 8 to 10 minutes | Serves 4

2 teaspoons honey	450 g baby carrots
1 teaspoon orange juice	2 teaspoons olive oil
½ teaspoon grated orange rind	¼ teaspoon salt
⅛ teaspoon ginger	

Combine honey, orange juice, grated rind, and ginger in a small bowl and set aside. Toss the carrots, oil, and salt together to coat well and pour them into the air fryer basket. Roast at 200ºC for 5 minutes. Shake basket to stir a little and cook for 2 to 4 minutes more, until carrots are barely tender. Pour carrots into a baking pan. Stir the honey mixture to combine well, pour glaze over carrots, and stir to coat. Roast at 180ºC for 1 minute or just until heated through.

Crispy Lemon Artichoke Hearts

Prep time: 10 minutes | Cook time: 15 minutes | Serves 2

1 (425 g) can artichoke hearts	30 g whole wheat bread crumbs
in water, drained	¼ teaspoon salt
1 egg	¼ teaspoon paprika
1 tablespoon water	½ lemon

Preheat the air fryer to 190ºC. In a medium shallow bowl, beat together the egg and water until frothy. In a separate medium shallow bowl, mix together the bread crumbs, salt, and paprika. Dip each artichoke heart into the egg mixture, then into the bread crumb mixture, coating the outside with the crumbs. Place the artichokes hearts in a single layer of the air fryer basket. Fry the artichoke hearts for 15 minutes. Remove the artichokes from the air fryer, and squeeze fresh lemon juice over the top before serving.

Citrus Sweet Potatoes and Carrots

Prep time: 5 minutes | Cook time: 20 to 25 minutes | Serves 4

2 large carrots, cut into 1-inch	2 garlic cloves, minced
chunks	2 tablespoons honey
1 medium sweet potato, peeled	1 tablespoon freshly squeezed
and cut into 1-inch cubes	orange juice
25 g chopped onion	2 teaspoons butter, melted

Insert the crisper plate into the basket and the basket into the unit. Preheat the unit by selecting AIR ROAST, setting the temperature to 200ºC, and setting the time to 3 minutes. Select START/STOP to begin. In a 6-by-2-inch round pan, toss together the carrots, sweet potato, onion, garlic, honey, orange juice, and melted butter to coat. Once the unit is preheated, place the pan into the basket. Select AIR ROAST, set the temperature to 200ºC, and set the time to 25 minutes. Select START/STOP to begin. After 15 minutes, remove the basket and shake the vegetables. Reinsert the basket to resume cooking. After 5 minutes, if the vegetables are tender and glazed, they are done. If not, resume cooking. When the cooking is complete, serve immediately.

Spicy Roasted Bok Choy

Prep time: 10 minutes | Cook time: 7 to 10 minutes | Serves 4

2 tablespoons olive oil	2 cloves garlic, minced
2 tablespoons reduced-sodium	1 head (about 450 g) bok choy,
coconut aminos	sliced lengthwise into quarters
2 teaspoons sesame oil	2 teaspoons black sesame seeds
2 teaspoons chili-garlic sauce	

Preheat the air fryer to 200ºC. In a large bowl, combine the olive oil, coconut aminos, sesame oil, chili-garlic sauce, and garlic. Add the bok choy and toss, massaging the leaves with your hands if necessary, until thoroughly coated. Arrange the bok choy in the basket of the air fryer. Pausing about halfway through the cooking time to shake the basket, air fry for 7 to 10 minutes until the bok choy is tender and the tips of the leaves begin to crisp. 4.Remove from the basket and let cool for a few minutes before coarsely chopping. Serve sprinkled with the sesame seeds.

Roasted Brussels Sprouts with Bacon

Prep time: 10 minutes | Cook time: 20 minutes | Serves 4

4 slices thick-cut bacon, chopped (about 110 g)	(or quartered if large)
450 g Brussels sprouts, halved	Freshly ground black pepper, to taste

Preheat the air fryer to 190ºC. Air fry the bacon for 5 minutes, shaking the basket once or twice during the cooking time. Add the Brussels sprouts to the basket and drizzle a little bacon fat from the bottom of the air fryer drawer into the basket. Toss the sprouts to coat with the bacon fat. Air fry for an additional 15 minutes, or until the Brussels sprouts are tender to a knifepoint. Season with freshly ground black pepper.

Baked Jalapeño and Cheese Cauliflower Mash

Prep time: 10 minutes | Cook time: 15 minutes | Serves 6

1 (340 g) steamer bag cauliflower florets, cooked according to package instructions	120 g shredded sharp Cheddar cheese
2 tablespoons salted butter, softened	20 g pickled jalapeños
	½ teaspoon salt
60 g cream cheese, softened	¼ teaspoon ground black pepper

Place cooked cauliflower into a food processor with remaining ingredients. Pulse twenty times until cauliflower is smooth and all ingredients are combined. Spoon mash into an ungreased round nonstick baking dish. Place dish into air fryer basket. Adjust the temperature to 190ºC and bake for 15 minutes. The top will be golden brown when done. Serve warm.

Mediterranean Courgette Boats

Prep time: 5 minutes | Cook time: 10 minutes | Serves 4

1 large courgette, ends removed, halved lengthwise	65 g feta cheese
6 grape tomatoes, quartered	1 tablespoon balsamic vinegar
¼ teaspoon salt	1 tablespoon olive oil

Use a spoon to scoop out 2 tablespoons from centre of each courgette half, making just enough space to fill with tomatoes and feta. Place tomatoes evenly in centres of courgette halves and sprinkle with salt. Place into ungreased air fryer basket. Adjust the temperature to 180ºC and roast for 10 minutes. When done, courgette will be tender. Transfer boats to a serving tray and sprinkle with feta, then drizzle with vinegar and olive oil. Serve warm.

Dill-and-Garlic Beetroots

Prep time: 10 minutes | Cook time: 30 minutes |
Serves 4

4 beetroots, cleaned, peeled, and sliced	dill
1 garlic clove, minced	¼ teaspoon salt
2 tablespoons chopped fresh	¼ teaspoon black pepper
	3 tablespoons olive oil

Preheat the air fryer to 190ºC. In a large bowl, mix together all of the ingredients so the beetroots are well coated with the oil. Pour the beetroot mixture into the air fryer basket, and roast for 15 minutes before stirring, then continue roasting for 15 minutes more.

Super Cheesy Gold Aubergine

Prep time: 15 minutes | Cook time: 30 minutes |
Serves 4

1 medium aubergine, peeled and cut into ½-inch-thick rounds	cheese
	Freshly ground black pepper, to taste
1 teaspoon salt, plus more for seasoning	Cooking oil spray
60 g plain flour	180 g marinara sauce
2 eggs	45 g shredded Parmesan cheese, divided
90 g Italian bread crumbs	110 g shredded Mozzarella cheese, divided
2 tablespoons grated Parmesan	

Blot the aubergine with paper towels to dry completely. You can also sprinkle with 1 teaspoon of salt to sweat out the moisture; if you do this, rinse the aubergine slices and blot dry again. Place the flour in a shallow bowl. In another shallow bowl, beat the eggs. In a third shallow bowl, stir together the bread crumbs and grated Parmesan cheese and season with salt and pepper. Dip each aubergine round in the flour, in the eggs, and into the bread crumbs to coat. Insert the crisper plate into the basket and the basket into the unit. Preheat the unit by selecting AIR FRY, setting the temperature to 200ºC, and setting the time to 3 minutes. Select START/STOP to begin. Once the unit is preheated, spray the crisper plate and the basket with cooking oil. Working in batches, place the aubergine rounds into the basket. Do not stack them. Spray the aubergine with the cooking oil. Select AIR FRY, set the temperature to 200ºC, and set the time to 10 minutes. Select START/STOP to begin. After 7 minutes, open the unit and top each round with 1 teaspoon of marinara sauce and ½ tablespoon each of shredded Parmesan and Mozzarella cheese. Resume cooking for 2 to 3 minutes until the cheese melts. 1Repeat steps 5, 6, 7, 8, and 9 with the remaining aubergine. 1When the cooking is complete, serve immediately.

Spinach and Sweet Pepper Poppers

Prep time: 10 minutes | Cook time: 8 minutes | Makes 16 poppers

110 g cream cheese, softened
20 g chopped fresh spinach leaves
½ teaspoon garlic powder

8 mini sweet bell peppers, tops removed, seeded, and halved lengthwise

In a medium bowl, mix cream cheese, spinach, and garlic powder. Place 1 tablespoon mixture into each sweet pepper half and press down to smooth. Place poppers into ungreased air fryer basket. Adjust the temperature to 200ºC and air fry for 8 minutes. Poppers will be done when cheese is browned on top and peppers are tender-crisp. Serve warm.

Caesar Whole Cauliflower

Prep time: 20 minutes | Cook time: 30 minutes | Serves 2 to 4

3 tablespoons olive oil
2 tablespoons red wine vinegar
2 tablespoons Worcestershire sauce
2 tablespoons grated Parmesan cheese
1 tablespoon Dijon mustard
4 garlic cloves, minced
4 oil-packed anchovy fillets,

drained and finely minced
coarse sea salt and freshly ground black pepper, to taste
1 small head cauliflower (about 450 g), green leaves trimmed and stem trimmed flush with the bottom of the head
1 tablespoon roughly chopped fresh flat-leaf parsley (optional)

In a liquid measuring jug, whisk together the olive oil, vinegar, Worcestershire, Parmesan, mustard, garlic, anchovies, and salt and pepper to taste. Place the cauliflower head upside down on a cutting board and use a paring knife to make an "x" through the full length of the core. Transfer the cauliflower head to a large bowl and pour half the dressing over it. Turn the cauliflower head to coat it in the dressing, then let it rest, stem-side up, in the dressing for at least 10 minutes and up to 30 minutes to allow the dressing to seep into all its nooks and crannies. Transfer the cauliflower head, stem-side down, to the air fryer and air fry at 170ºC or 25 minutes. Drizzle the remaining dressing over the cauliflower and air fry at 200ºC until the top of the cauliflower is golden brown and the core is tender, about 5 minutes more. Remove the basket from the air fryer and transfer the cauliflower to a large plate. Sprinkle with the parsley, if you like, and serve hot.

Spiced Butternut Squash

Prep time: 10 minutes | Cook time: 15 minutes | Serves 4

600 g 1-inch-cubed butternut squash
2 tablespoons vegetable oil

1 to 2 tablespoons brown sugar
1 teaspoon Chinese five-spice powder

In a medium bowl, combine the squash, oil, sugar, and five-spice powder. Toss to coat. Place the squash in the air fryer basket. Set the air fryer to 200ºC for 15 minutes or until tender.

Fried Brussels Sprouts

Prep time: 10 minutes | Cook time: 18 minutes | Serves 4

1 teaspoon plus 1 tablespoon extra-virgin olive oil, divided
2 teaspoons minced garlic
2 tablespoons honey
1 tablespoon sugar
2 tablespoons freshly squeezed lemon juice
2 tablespoons rice vinegar

2 tablespoons sriracha
450 g Brussels sprouts, stems trimmed and any tough leaves removed, rinsed, halved lengthwise, and dried
½ teaspoon salt
Cooking oil spray

In a small saucepan over low heat, combine 1 teaspoon of olive oil, the garlic, honey, sugar, lemon juice, vinegar, and sriracha. Cook for 2 to 3 minutes, or until slightly thickened. Remove the pan from the heat, cover, and set aside. Place the Brussels sprouts in a resealable bag or small bowl. Add the remaining olive oil and the salt, and toss to coat. Insert the crisper plate into the basket and the basket into the unit. Preheat the unit by selecting AIR FRY, setting the temperature to 200ºC, and setting the time to 3 minutes. Select START/STOP to begin. Once the unit is preheated, spray the crisper plate with cooking oil. Add the Brussels sprouts to the basket. Select AIR FRY, set the temperature to 200ºC, and set the time to 15 minutes. Select START/STOP to begin. After 7 or 8 minutes, remove the basket and shake it to toss the sprouts. Reinsert the basket to resume cooking. When the cooking is complete, the leaves should be crispy and light brown and the sprout centres tender. Place the sprouts in a medium serving bowl and drizzle the sauce over the top. Toss to coat, and serve immediately.

Chapter 6 Poultry

Yakitori

Prep time: 10 minutes | Cook time: 15 minutes | Serves 4

120 ml mirin
60 ml dry white wine
120 ml soy sauce
1 tablespoon light brown sugar
680 g boneless, skinless chicken thighs, cut into 1½-inch pieces, fat trimmed
4 medium spring onions,
trimmed, cut into 1½-inch pieces
Cooking spray
Special Equipment:
4 (4-inch) bamboo skewers, soaked in water for at least 30 minutes

Combine the mirin, dry white wine, soy sauce, and brown sugar in a saucepan. Bring to a boil over medium heat. Keep stirring. Boil for another 2 minutes or until it has a thick consistency. Turn off the heat. Preheat the air fryer to 200ºC. Spritz the air fryer basket with cooking spray. Run the bamboo skewers through the chicken pieces and spring onions alternatively. Arrange the skewers in the preheated air fryer, then brush with mirin mixture on both sides. Spritz with cooking spray. Air fry for 10 minutes or until the chicken and spring onions are glossy. Flip the skewers halfway through. Serve immediately.

Broccoli and Cheese Stuffed Chicken

Prep time: 15 minutes | Cook time: 20 minutes | Serves 4

60 g cream cheese, softened
70 g chopped fresh broccoli, steamed
120 g shredded sharp Cheddar cheese
4 (170 g) boneless, skinless
chicken breasts
2 tablespoons mayonnaise
¼ teaspoon salt
¼ teaspoon garlic powder
⅛ teaspoon ground black pepper

In a medium bowl, combine cream cheese, broccoli, and Cheddar. Cut a 4-inch pocket into each chicken breast. Evenly divide mixture between chicken breasts; stuff the pocket of each chicken breast with the mixture. Spread ¼ tablespoon mayonnaise per side of each chicken breast, then sprinkle both sides of breasts with salt, garlic powder, and pepper. Place stuffed chicken breasts into ungreased air fryer basket so that the open seams face up. Adjust the temperature to 180ºC and air fry for 20 minutes, turning chicken halfway through cooking. When done, chicken will be golden and have an internal temperature of at least 75ºC. Serve warm.

Golden Tenders

Prep time: 10 minutes | Cook time: 15 minutes | Serves 4

120 g panko bread crumbs
1 tablespoon paprika
½ teaspoon salt
¼ teaspoon freshly ground
black pepper
16 chicken tenders
115 g mayonnaise
Olive oil spray

In a medium bowl, stir together the panko, paprika, salt, and pepper. In a large bowl, toss together the chicken tenders and mayonnaise to coat. Transfer the coated chicken pieces to the bowl of seasoned panko and dredge to coat thoroughly. Press the coating onto the chicken with your fingers. Insert the crisper plate into the basket and the basket into the unit. Preheat the unit by selecting AIR FRY, setting the temperature to 180ºC, and setting the time to 3 minutes. Select START/STOP to begin. Once the unit is preheated, place a parchment paper liner into the basket. Place the chicken into the basket and spray it with olive oil. Select AIR FRY, set the temperature to 180ºC, and set the time to 15 minutes. Select START/STOP to begin. When the cooking is complete, the tenders will be golden brown and a food thermometer inserted into the chicken should register 75ºC. For more even browning, remove the basket halfway through cooking and flip the tenders. Give them an extra spray of olive oil and reinsert the basket to resume cooking. This ensures they are crispy and brown all over. When the cooking is complete, serve.

Chipotle Drumsticks

Prep time: 15 minutes | Cook time: 20 minutes | Serves 4

1 tablespoon tomato paste
½ teaspoon chipotle powder
¼ teaspoon apple cider vinegar
¼ teaspoon garlic powder
8 chicken drumsticks
½ teaspoon salt
⅛ teaspoon ground black pepper

In a small bowl, combine tomato paste, chipotle powder, vinegar, and garlic powder. Sprinkle drumsticks with salt and pepper, then place into a large bowl and pour in tomato paste mixture. Toss or stir to evenly coat all drumsticks in mixture. Place drumsticks into ungreased air fryer basket. Adjust the temperature to 200ºC and air fry for 25 minutes, turning drumsticks halfway through cooking. Drumsticks will be dark red with an internal temperature of at least 75ºC when done. Serve warm.

Buttermilk Breaded Chicken

Prep time: 7 minutes | Cook time: 20 to 25 minutes | Serves 4

125 g all-purpose flour	2 tablespoons extra-virgin olive
2 teaspoons paprika	oil
Pinch salt	185 g bread crumbs
Freshly ground black pepper, to	6 chicken pieces, drumsticks,
taste	breasts, and thighs, patted dry
80 ml buttermilk	Cooking oil spray
2 eggs	

In a shallow bowl, stir together the flour, paprika, salt, and pepper. In another bowl, beat the buttermilk and eggs until smooth. In a third bowl, stir together the olive oil and bread crumbs until mixed. Dredge the chicken in the flour, dip in the eggs to coat, and finally press into the bread crumbs, patting the crumbs firmly onto the chicken skin. Insert the crisper plate into the basket and the basket into the unit. Preheat the unit by selecting AIR FRY, setting the temperature to 190ºC, and setting the time to 3 minutes. Select START/STOP to begin. Once the unit is preheated, spray the crisper plate with cooking oil. Place the chicken into the basket. Select AIR FRY, set the temperature to 190ºC, and set the time to 25 minutes. Select START/STOP to begin. After 10 minutes, flip the chicken. Resume cooking. After 10 minutes more, check the chicken. If a food thermometer inserted into the chicken registers 75ºC and the chicken is brown and crisp, it is done. Otherwise, resume cooking for up to 5 minutes longer. When the cooking is complete, let cool for 5 minutes, then serve.

Chicken Burgers with Ham and Cheese

Prep time: 12 minutes | Cook time: 13 to 16 minutes | Serves 4

40 g soft bread crumbs	taste
3 tablespoons milk	570 g chicken mince
1 egg, beaten	70 g finely chopped ham
½ teaspoon dried thyme	75 g grated Gouda cheese
Pinch salt	Olive oil for misting
Freshly ground black pepper, to	

Preheat the air fryer to 180ºC. In a medium bowl, combine the bread crumbs, milk, egg, thyme, salt, and pepper. Add the chicken and mix gently but thoroughly with clean hands. Form the chicken into eight thin patties and place on waxed paper. Top four of the patties with the ham and cheese. Top with remaining four patties and gently press the edges together to seal, so the ham and cheese mixture is in the middle of the burger. Place the burgers in the basket and mist with olive oil. Bake for 13 to 16 minutes or until the chicken is thoroughly cooked to 75ºC as measured with a meat thermometer. Serve immediately.

Spice-Rubbed Chicken Thighs

Prep time: 10 minutes | Cook time: 25 minutes | Serves 4

4 (115 g) bone-in, skin-on	2 teaspoons chili powder
chicken thighs	1 teaspoon paprika
½ teaspoon salt	1 teaspoon ground cumin
½ teaspoon garlic powder	1 small lime, halved

Pat chicken thighs dry and sprinkle with salt, garlic powder, chili powder, paprika, and cumin. Squeeze juice from ½ lime over thighs. Place thighs into ungreased air fryer basket. Adjust the temperature to 190ºC and roast for 25 minutes, turning thighs halfway through cooking. Thighs will be crispy and browned with an internal temperature of at least 75ºC when done. Transfer thighs to a large serving plate and drizzle with remaining lime juice. Serve warm.

Classic Chicken Kebab

Prep time: 35 minutes | Cook time: 25 minutes | Serves 4

60 ml olive oil	450 g boneless skinless chicken
1 teaspoon garlic powder	thighs, cut into 1-inch pieces
1 teaspoon onion powder	1 red bell pepper, cut into 1-inch
1 teaspoon ground cumin	pieces
½ teaspoon dried oregano	1 red onion, cut into 1-inch
½ teaspoon dried basil	pieces
60 ml lemon juice	1 courgette, cut into 1-inch
1 tablespoon apple cider	pieces
vinegar	12 cherry tomatoes
Olive oil cooking spray	

In a large bowl, mix together the olive oil, garlic powder, onion powder, cumin, oregano, basil, lemon juice, and apple cider vinegar. Spray six skewers with olive oil cooking spray. On each skewer, slide on a piece of chicken, then a piece of bell pepper, onion, courgette, and finally a tomato and then repeat. Each skewer should have at least two pieces of each item. Once all of the skewers are prepared, place them in a 9-by-13-inch baking dish and pour the olive oil marinade over the top of the skewers. Turn each skewer so that all sides of the chicken and vegetables are coated. Cover the dish with plastic wrap and place it in the refrigerator for 30 minutes. After 30 minutes, preheat the air fryer to 190ºC. (If using a grill attachment, make sure it is inside the air fryer during preheating.) Remove the skewers from the marinade and lay them in a single layer in the air fryer basket. If the air fryer has a grill attachment, you can also lay them on this instead. Cook for 10 minutes. Rotate the kebabs, then cook them for 15 minutes more. Remove the skewers from the air fryer and let them rest for 5 minutes before serving.

Garlic Dill Wings

Prep time: 5 minutes | Cook time: 25 minutes | Serves 4

900 g bone-in chicken wings, separated at joints	pepper
½ teaspoon salt	½ teaspoon onion powder
½ teaspoon ground black	½ teaspoon garlic powder
	1 teaspoon dried dill

In a large bowl, toss wings with salt, pepper, onion powder, garlic powder, and dill until evenly coated. Place wings into ungreased air fryer basket in a single layer, working in batches if needed. Adjust the temperature to 200°C and air fry for 25 minutes, shaking the basket every 7 minutes during cooking. Wings should have an internal temperature of at least 75°C and be golden brown when done. Serve warm.

Hoisin Turkey Burgers

Prep time: 30 minutes | Cook time: 20 minutes | Serves 4

Olive oil	60 ml hoisin sauce
450 g lean turkey mince	2 tablespoons soy sauce
30 g whole-wheat bread crumbs	4 whole-wheat buns

Spray the air fryer basket lightly with olive oil. In a large bowl, mix together the turkey, bread crumbs, hoisin sauce, and soy sauce. Form the mixture into 4 equal patties. Cover with plastic wrap and refrigerate the patties for 30 minutes. Place the patties in the air fryer basket in a single layer. Spray the patties lightly with olive oil. Air fry at 190°C for 10 minutes. Flip the patties over, lightly spray with olive oil, and cook until golden brown, an additional 5 to 10 minutes. Place the patties on buns and top with your choice of low-calorie burger toppings like sliced tomatoes, onions, and cabbage slaw.

Honey-Glazed Chicken Thighs

Prep time: 5 minutes | Cook time: 14 minutes | Serves 4

Oil, for spraying	1 tablespoon balsamic vinegar
4 boneless, skinless chicken thighs, fat trimmed	2 teaspoons honey
3 tablespoons soy sauce	2 teaspoons minced garlic
	1 teaspoon ground ginger

Preheat the air fryer to 200°C. Line the air fryer basket with parchment and spray lightly with oil. Place the chicken in the prepared basket. Cook for 7 minutes, flip, and cook for another 7 minutes, or until the internal temperature reaches 75°C and the juices run clear. In a small saucepan, combine the soy sauce, balsamic vinegar, honey, garlic, and ginger and cook over low heat for 1 to 2 minutes, until warmed through. Transfer the chicken to a serving plate and drizzle with the sauce just before serving.

Brazilian Tempero Baiano Chicken Drumsticks

Prep time: 30 minutes | Cook time: 20 minutes | Serves 4

1 teaspoon cumin seeds	½ teaspoon black peppercorns
1 teaspoon dried oregano	½ teaspoon cayenne pepper
1 teaspoon dried parsley	60 ml fresh lime juice
1 teaspoon ground turmeric	2 tablespoons olive oil
½ teaspoon coriander seeds	680 g chicken drumsticks
1 teaspoon kosher salt	

In a clean coffee grinder or spice mill, combine the cumin, oregano, parsley, turmeric, coriander seeds, salt, peppercorns, and cayenne. Process until finely ground. In a small bowl, combine the ground spices with the lime juice and oil. Place the chicken in a resealable plastic bag. Add the marinade, seal, and massage until the chicken is well coated. Marinate at room temperature for 30 minutes or in the refrigerator for up to 24 hours. When you are ready to cook, place the drumsticks skin side up in the air fryer basket. Set the air fryer to 200°C for 20 to 25 minutes, turning the legs halfway through the cooking time. Use a meat thermometer to ensure that the chicken has reached an internal temperature of 75°C. Serve with plenty of napkins.

Fried Chicken Breasts

Prep time: 30 minutes | Cook time: 12 to 14 minutes | Serves 4

450 g boneless, skinless chicken breasts	cheese
180 ml dill pickle juice	½ teaspoon sea salt
70 g finely ground blanched almond flour	½ teaspoon freshly ground black pepper
70 g finely grated Parmesan	2 large eggs
	Avocado oil spray

Place the chicken breasts in a zip-top bag or between two pieces of plastic wrap. Using a meat mallet or heavy skillet, pound the chicken to a uniform ½-inch thickness. Place the chicken in a large bowl with the pickle juice. Cover and allow to brine in the refrigerator for up to 2 hours. In a shallow dish, combine the almond flour, Parmesan cheese, salt, and pepper. In a separate, shallow bowl, beat the eggs. Drain the chicken and pat it dry with paper towels. Dip in the eggs and then in the flour mixture, making sure to press the coating into the chicken. Spray both sides of the coated breasts with oil. Spray the air fryer basket with oil and put the chicken inside. Set the temperature to 200°C and air fry for 6 to 7 minutes. Carefully flip the breasts with a spatula. Spray the breasts again with oil and continue cooking for 6 to 7 minutes more, until golden and crispy.

Wild Rice and Kale Stuffed Chicken Thighs

Prep time: 10 minutes | Cook time: 22 minutes | Serves 4

4 boneless, skinless chicken thighs	1 teaspoon salt
250 g cooked wild rice	Juice of 1 lemon
35 g chopped kale	100 g crumbled feta
2 garlic cloves, minced	Olive oil cooking spray
	1 tablespoon olive oi

Preheat the air fryer to 190ºC. Place the chicken thighs between two pieces of plastic wrap, and using a meat mallet or a rolling pin, pound them out to about ¼-inch thick. In a medium bowl, combine the rice, kale, garlic, salt, and lemon juice and mix well. Place a quarter of the rice mixture into the middle of each chicken thigh, then sprinkle 2 tablespoons of feta over the filling. Spray the air fryer basket with olive oil cooking spray. Fold the sides of the chicken thigh over the filling, and then gently place each of them seam-side down into the air fryer basket. Brush each stuffed chicken thigh with olive oil. Roast the stuffed chicken thighs for 12 minutes, then turn them over and cook for an additional 10 minutes, or until the internal temperature reaches 75ºC.

Peanut Butter Chicken Satay

Prep time: 12 minutes | Cook time: 12 to 18 minutes | Serves 4

120 g crunchy peanut butter	2 garlic cloves, minced
80 ml chicken broth	2 tablespoons extra-virgin olive oil
3 tablespoons low-sodium soy sauce	1 teaspoon curry powder
2 tablespoons freshly squeezed lemon juice	450 g chicken tenders
	Cooking oil spray

In a medium bowl, whisk the peanut butter, broth, soy sauce, lemon juice, garlic, olive oil, and curry powder until smooth. Place 2 tablespoons of this mixture into a small bowl. Transfer the remaining sauce to a serving bowl and set aside. Add the chicken tenders to the bowl with the 2 tablespoons of sauce and stir to coat. Let stand for a few minutes to marinate. Insert the crisper plate into the basket and the basket into the unit. Preheat the unit by selecting AIR FRY, setting the temperature to 200ºC, and setting the time to 3 minutes. Select START/STOP to begin. Run a 6-inch bamboo skewer lengthwise through each chicken tender. Once the unit is preheated, spray the crisper plate with cooking oil. Working in batches, place half the chicken skewers into the basket in a single layer without overlapping. Select AIR FRY, set the temperature to 200ºC, and set the time to 9 minutes. Select START/STOP to begin. After 6 minutes, check the chicken. If a food thermometer inserted into the chicken registers 75ºC, it is done. If not, resume cooking. Repeat steps 6, 7, and 8 with the remaining chicken. 1When the cooking is complete, serve the chicken with the reserved sauce.

Chicken Pesto Pizzas

Prep time: 10 minutes | Cook time: 12 minutes | Serves 4

450 g chicken mince thighs	20 g basil pesto
¼ teaspoon salt	225 g shredded Mozzarella cheese
⅛ teaspoon ground black pepper	4 grape tomatoes, sliced

Cut four squares of parchment paper to fit into your air fryer basket. Place chicken mince in a large bowl and mix with salt and pepper. Divide mixture into four equal sections. Wet your hands with water to prevent sticking, then press each section into a 6-inch circle onto a piece of ungreased parchment. Place each chicken crust into air fryer basket, working in batches if needed. Adjust the temperature to 180ºC and air fry for 10 minutes, turning crusts halfway through cooking. Spread 1 tablespoon pesto across the top of each crust, then sprinkle with ¼ of the Mozzarella and top with 1 sliced tomato. Continue cooking at 180ºC for 2 minutes. Cheese will be melted and brown when done. Serve warm.

Porchetta-Style Chicken Breasts

Prep time: 10 minutes | Cook time: 15 minutes | Serves 4

25 g fresh parsley leaves	1 teaspoon ground fennel
10 g roughly chopped fresh chives	½ teaspoon red pepper flakes
4 cloves garlic, peeled	4 (115 g) boneless, skinless chicken breasts, pounded to ¼ inch thick
2 tablespoons lemon juice	
3 teaspoons fine sea salt	8 slices bacon
1 teaspoon dried rubbed sage	Sprigs of fresh rosemary, for garnish (optional)
1 teaspoon fresh rosemary leaves	

Spray the air fryer basket with avocado oil. Preheat the air fryer to 170ºC. Place the parsley, chives, garlic, lemon juice, salt, sage, rosemary, fennel, and red pepper flakes in a food processor and purée until a smooth paste forms. Place the chicken breasts on a cutting board and rub the paste all over the tops. With a short end facing you, roll each breast up like a jelly roll to make a log and secure it with toothpicks. Wrap 2 slices of bacon around each chicken breast log to cover the entire breast. Secure the bacon with toothpicks. Place the chicken breast logs in the air fryer basket and air fry for 5 minutes, flip the logs over, and cook for another 5 minutes. Increase the heat to 200ºC and cook until the bacon is crisp, about 5 minutes more. Remove the toothpicks and garnish with fresh rosemary sprigs, if desired, before serving. Store leftovers in an airtight container in the refrigerator for up to 4 days or in the freezer for up to a month. Reheat in a preheated 180ºC air fryer for 5 minutes, then increase the heat to 200ºC and cook for 2 minutes to crisp the bacon.

Nice Goulash

Prep time: 5 minutes | Cook time: 17 minutes | Serves 2

2 red bell peppers, chopped	Salt and ground black pepper,
450 g chicken mince	to taste
2 medium tomatoes, diced	Cooking spray
120 ml chicken broth	

Preheat the air fryer to 185°C. Spritz a baking pan with cooking spray. Set the bell pepper in the baking pan and put in the air fry to broil for 5 minutes or until the bell pepper is tender. Shake the basket halfway through. Add the chicken mince and diced tomatoes in the baking pan and stir to mix well. Broil for 6 more minutes or until the chicken is lightly browned. Pour the chicken broth over and sprinkle with salt and ground black pepper. Stir to mix well. Broil for an additional 6 minutes. Serve immediately.

Breaded Turkey Cutlets

Prep time: 5 minutes | Cook time: 8 minutes | Serves 4

60 g whole wheat bread crumbs	⅛ teaspoon garlic powder
¼ teaspoon paprika	1 egg
¼ teaspoon salt	4 turkey breast cutlets
¼ teaspoon black pepper	Chopped fresh parsley, for
⅛ teaspoon dried sage	serving

Preheat the air fryer to 190°C. In a medium shallow bowl, whisk together the bread crumbs, paprika, salt, black pepper, sage, and garlic powder. In a separate medium shallow bowl, whisk the egg until frothy. Dip each turkey cutlet into the egg mixture, then into the bread crumb mixture, coating the outside with the crumbs. Place the breaded turkey cutlets in a single layer in the bottom of the air fryer basket, making sure that they don't touch each other. Bake for 4 minutes. Turn the cutlets over, then bake for 4 minutes more, or until the internal temperature reaches 75°C. Sprinkle on the parsley and serve.

Ginger Turmeric Chicken Thighs

Prep time: 5 minutes | Cook time: 25 minutes | Serves 4

4 (115 g) boneless, skin-on	½ teaspoon salt
chicken thighs	½ teaspoon garlic powder
2 tablespoons coconut oil,	½ teaspoon ground ginger
melted	¼ teaspoon ground black
½ teaspoon ground turmeric	pepper

Place chicken thighs in a large bowl and drizzle with coconut oil. Sprinkle with remaining ingredients and toss to coat both sides of thighs. Place thighs skin side up into ungreased air fryer basket. Adjust the temperature to 200°C and air fry for 25 minutes. After 10 minutes, turn thighs. When 5 minutes remain, flip thighs once more. Chicken will be done when skin is golden brown and the internal temperature is at least 75°C. Serve warm.

Chicken and Vegetable Fajitas

Prep time: 15 minutes | Cook time: 23 minutes | Serves 6

Chicken:	1 tablespoon vegetable oil
450 g boneless, skinless chicken	½ teaspoon kosher salt
thighs, cut crosswise into thirds	½ teaspoon ground cumin
1 tablespoon vegetable oil	For Serving:
4½ teaspoons taco seasoning	Tortillas
Vegetables:	Sour cream
50 g sliced onion	Shredded cheese
150 g sliced bell pepper	Guacamole
1 or 2 jalapeños, quartered	Salsa
lengthwise	

For the chicken: In a medium bowl, toss together the chicken, vegetable oil, and taco seasoning to coat. For the vegetables: In a separate bowl, toss together the onion, bell pepper, jalapeño(s), vegetable oil, salt, and cumin to coat. Place the chicken in the air fryer basket. Set the air fryer to (190°C for 10 minutes. Add the vegetables to the basket, toss everything together to blend the seasonings, and set the air fryer for 13 minutes more. Use a meat thermometer to ensure the chicken has reached an internal temperature of 75°C. Transfer the chicken and vegetables to a serving platter. Serve with tortillas and the desired fajita fixings.

Turkey Meatloaf

Prep time: 10 minutes | Cook time: 50 minutes | Serves 4

230 g sliced mushrooms	2 tablespoons almond milk
1 small onion, coarsely chopped	1 tablespoon dried oregano
2 cloves garlic	1 teaspoon salt
680 g 85% lean turkey mince	½ teaspoon freshly ground
2 eggs, lightly beaten	black pepper
1 tablespoon tomato paste	1 Roma tomato, thinly sliced
25 g almond meal	

Preheat the air fryer to 180°C. . Lightly coat a round pan with olive oil and set aside. In a food processor fitted with a metal blade, combine the mushrooms, onion, and garlic. Pulse until finely chopped. Transfer the vegetables to a large mixing bowl. Add the turkey, eggs, tomato paste, almond meal, milk, oregano, salt, and black pepper. Mix gently until thoroughly combined. Transfer the mixture to the prepared pan and shape into a loaf. Arrange the tomato slices on top. Air fry for 50 minutes or until the meatloaf is nicely browned and a thermometer inserted into the thickest part registers 75°C. Remove from the air fryer and let rest for about 10 minutes before slicing.

Greek Chicken Stir-Fry

Prep time: 15 minutes | Cook time: 15 minutes | Serves 2

1 (170 g) chicken breast, cut into 1-inch cubes
½ medium courgette, chopped
½ medium red bell pepper, seeded and chopped
¼ medium red onion, peeled
and sliced
1 tablespoon coconut oil
1 teaspoon dried oregano
½ teaspoon garlic powder
¼ teaspoon dried thyme

Place all ingredients into a large mixing bowl and toss until the coconut oil coats the meat and vegetables. Pour the contents of the bowl into the air fryer basket. Adjust the temperature to (190ºC and air fry for 15 minutes. Shake the basket halfway through the cooking time to redistribute the food. Serve immediately.

Lemon-Basil Turkey Breasts

Prep time: 30 minutes | Cook time: 58 minutes | Serves 4

2 tablespoons olive oil
900 g turkey breasts, bone-in, skin-on
Coarse sea salt and ground black pepper, to taste
1 teaspoon fresh basil leaves, chopped
2 tablespoons lemon zest, grated

Rub olive oil on all sides of the turkey breasts; sprinkle with salt, pepper, basil, and lemon zest. Place the turkey breasts skin side up on the parchment-lined air fryer basket. Cook in the preheated air fryer at 170ºC for 30 minutes. Now, turn them over and cook an additional 28 minutes. Serve with lemon wedges, if desired. Bon appétit!

Buffalo Crispy Chicken Strips

Prep time: 15 minutes | Cook time: 13 to 17 minutes per batch | Serves 4

90 g all-purpose flour
2 eggs
2 tablespoons water
120 g seasoned panko bread crumbs
2 teaspoons granulated garlic
1 teaspoon salt
1 teaspoon freshly ground black
pepper
16 chicken breast strips, or 3 large boneless, skinless chicken breasts, cut into 1-inch strips
Olive oil spray
60 ml Buffalo sauce, plus more as needed

Put the flour in a small bowl. In another small bowl, whisk the eggs and the water. In a third bowl, stir together the panko, granulated garlic, salt, and pepper. Dip each chicken strip in the flour, in the egg, and in the panko mixture to coat. Press the crumbs onto the chicken with your fingers. Insert the crisper plate into the basket and the basket into the unit. Preheat the unit by selecting AIR FRY, setting the temperature to 190ºC, and setting the time to 3 minutes. Select START/STOP to begin. Once the unit is preheated, place a parchment paper liner into the basket. Working in batches if needed, place the chicken strips into the basket. Do not stack unless using a wire rack for the second layer. Spray the top of the chicken with olive oil. Select AIR FRY, set the temperature to 190ºC, and set the time to 17 minutes. Select START/STOP to begin. After 10 or 12 minutes, remove the basket, flip the chicken, and spray again with olive oil. Reinsert the basket to resume cooking. When the cooking is complete, the chicken should be golden brown and crispy and a food thermometer inserted into the chicken should register 75ºC. 1Repeat steps 6, 7, and 8 with any remaining chicken. 1Transfer the chicken to a large bowl. Drizzle the Buffalo sauce over the top of the cooked chicken, toss to coat, and serve.

Teriyaki Chicken Thighs with Lemony Snow Peas

Prep time: 30 minutes | Cook time: 34 minutes | Serves 4

60 ml chicken broth
½ teaspoon grated fresh ginger
⅛ teaspoon red pepper flakes
1½ tablespoons soy sauce
4 (140 g) bone-in chicken thighs, trimmed
1 tablespoon mirin
½ teaspoon cornflour
1 tablespoon sugar
170 g mangetout, strings removed
⅛ teaspoon lemon zest
1 garlic clove, minced
¼ teaspoon salt
Ground black pepper, to taste
½ teaspoon lemon juice

Combine the broth, ginger, pepper flakes, and soy sauce in a large bowl. Stir to mix well. Pierce 10 to 15 holes into the chicken skin. Put the chicken in the broth mixture and toss to coat well. Let sit for 10 minutes to marinate. Preheat the air fryer to 205ºC. Transfer the marinated chicken on a plate and pat dry with paper towels. Scoop 2 tablespoons of marinade in a microwave-safe bowl and combine with mirin, cornflour and sugar. Stir to mix well. Microwave for 1 minute or until frothy and has a thick consistency. Set aside. Arrange the chicken in the preheated air fryer, skin side up, and air fry for 25 minutes or until the internal temperature of the chicken reaches at least 75ºC. Gently turn the chicken over halfway through. When the frying is complete, brush the chicken skin with marinade mixture. Air fryer the chicken for 5 more minutes or until glazed. Remove the chicken from the air fryer and reserve ½ teaspoon of chicken fat remains in the air fryer. Allow the chicken to cool for 10 minutes. Meanwhile, combine the reserved chicken fat, snow peas, lemon zest, garlic, salt, and ground black pepper in a small bowl. Toss to coat well. 1Transfer the snow peas in the air fryer and air fry for 3 minutes or until soft. Remove the peas from the air fryer and toss with lemon juice. 1Serve the chicken with lemony snow peas.

Chicken with Bacon and Tomato

Prep time: 25 minutes | Cook time: 10 minutes | Serves 4

4 medium-sized skin-on chicken drumsticks	2 tablespoons olive oil
1½ teaspoons herbs de Provence	2 garlic cloves, crushed
	340 g crushed canned tomatoes
Salt and pepper, to taste	1 small-size leek, thinly sliced
1 tablespoon rice vinegar	2 slices smoked bacon, chopped

Sprinkle the chicken drumsticks with herbs de Provence, salt and pepper; then, drizzle them with rice vinegar and olive oil. Cook in the baking pan at 180°C for 8 to 10 minutes. Pause the air fryer; stir in the remaining ingredients and continue to cook for 15 minutes longer; make sure to check them periodically. Bon appétit!

Ham Chicken with Cheese

Prep time: 15 minutes | Cook time: 25 minutes | Serves 4

55 g unsalted butter, softened	60 ml water
115 g cream cheese, softened	280 g shredded cooked chicken
1½ teaspoons Dijon mustard	115 g ham, chopped
2 tablespoons white wine vinegar	115 g sliced Swiss or Provolone cheese

Preheat the air fryer to 190°C. Lightly coat a casserole dish that will fit in the air fryer, such as an 8-inch round pan, with olive oil and set aside. In a large bowl and using an electric mixer, combine the butter, cream cheese, Dijon mustard, and vinegar. With the motor running at low speed, slowly add the water and beat until smooth. Set aside. Arrange an even layer of chicken in the bottom of the prepared pan, followed by the ham. Spread the butter and cream cheese mixture on top of the ham, followed by the cheese slices on the top layer. Air fry for 20 to 25 minutes until warmed through and the cheese has browned.

Herbed Turkey Breast with Simple Dijon Sauce

Prep time: 5 minutes | Cook time: 30 minutes | Serves 4

1 teaspoon chopped fresh sage	1½ teaspoons sea salt
1 teaspoon chopped fresh tarragon	1 teaspoon ground black pepper
	1 (900 g) turkey breast
1 teaspoon chopped fresh thyme leaves	3 tablespoons Dijon mustard
	3 tablespoons butter, melted
1 teaspoon chopped fresh rosemary leaves	Cooking spray

Preheat the air fryer to 200°C. Spritz the air fryer basket with cooking spray. Combine the herbs, salt, and black pepper in a small bowl. Stir to mix well. Set aside. Combine the Dijon mustard and butter in a separate bowl. Stir to mix well. Rub the turkey with the herb mixture on a clean work surface, then brush the turkey with Dijon mixture. Arrange the turkey in the preheated air fryer basket. Air fry for 30 minutes or until an instant-read thermometer inserted in the thickest part of the turkey breast reaches at least 75°C. Transfer the cooked turkey breast on a large plate and slice to serve.

Classic Whole Chicken

Prep time: 5 minutes | Cook time: 50 minutes | Serves 4

Oil, for spraying	½ teaspoon salt
1 (1.8 kg) whole chicken, giblets removed	½ teaspoon freshly ground black pepper
1 tablespoon olive oil	¼ teaspoon finely chopped fresh parsley, for garnish
1 teaspoon paprika	
½ teaspoon granulated garlic	

Line the air fryer basket with parchment and spray lightly with oil. Pat the chicken dry with paper towels. Rub it with the olive oil until evenly coated. In a small bowl, mix together the paprika, garlic, salt, and black pepper and sprinkle it evenly over the chicken. Place the chicken in the prepared basket, breast-side down. Air fry at 180°C for 30 minutes, flip, and cook for another 20 minutes, or until the internal temperature reaches 75°C and the juices run clear. Sprinkle with the parsley before serving.

Chicken Parmesan

Prep time: 15 minutes | Cook time: 10 minutes | Serves 4

Oil, for spraying	plus 45 g shredded
2 (230 g) boneless, skinless chicken breasts	4 tablespoons unsalted butter, melted
120 g Italian-style bread crumbs	115 g marinara sauce
20 g grated Parmesan cheese,	

Preheat the air fryer to 180°C. Line the air fryer basket with parchment and spray lightly with oil. Cut each chicken breast in half through its thickness to make 4 thin cutlets. Using a meat tenderizer, pound each cutlet until it is about ¾ inch thick. On a plate, mix together the bread crumbs and grated Parmesan cheese. Lightly brush the chicken with the melted butter, then dip into the bread crumb mixture. Place the chicken in the prepared basket and spray lightly with oil. You may need to work in batches, depending on the size of your air fryer. Cook for 6 minutes. Top the chicken with the marinara and shredded Parmesan cheese, dividing evenly. Cook for another 3 to 4 minutes, or until golden brown, crispy, and the internal temperature reaches 75°C.

Chicken Thighs with Coriander

Prep time: 15 minutes | Cook time: 25 minutes | Serves 4

1 tablespoon olive oil	8 bone-in chicken thighs, skin
Juice of ½ lime	on
1 tablespoon coconut aminos	2 tablespoons chopped fresh
1½ teaspoons Montreal chicken seasoning	coriander

In a gallon-size resealable bag, combine the olive oil, lime juice, coconut aminos, and chicken seasoning. Add the chicken thighs, seal the bag, and massage the bag to ensure the chicken is thoroughly coated. Refrigerate for at least 2 hours, preferably overnight. Preheat the air fryer to 200°C. Remove the chicken from the marinade (discard the marinade) and arrange in a single layer in the air fryer basket. Pausing halfway through the cooking time to flip the chicken, air fry for 20 to 25 minutes, until a thermometer inserted into the thickest part registers 75°C. Transfer the chicken to a serving platter and top with the coriander before serving.

Chicken Pesto Parmigiana

Prep time: 10 minutes | Cook time: 23 minutes | Serves 4

2 large eggs	pounded to ¼ inch thick
1 tablespoon water	65 g pesto
Fine sea salt and ground black pepper, to taste	115 g shredded Mozzarella cheese
85 g powdered Parmesan cheese	Finely chopped fresh basil, for garnish (optional)
2 teaspoons Italian seasoning	Grape tomatoes, halved, for serving (optional)
4 (140 g) boneless, skinless chicken breasts or thighs,	

Spray the air fryer basket with avocado oil. Preheat the air fryer to 200°C. Crack the eggs into a shallow baking dish, add the water and a pinch each of salt and pepper, and whisk to combine. In another shallow baking dish, stir together the Parmesan and Italian seasoning until well combined. Season the chicken breasts well on both sides with salt and pepper. Dip one chicken breast in the eggs and let any excess drip off, then dredge both sides of the breast in the Parmesan mixture. Spray the breast with avocado oil and place it in the air fryer basket. Repeat with the remaining 3 chicken breasts. Air fry the chicken in the air fryer for 20 minutes, or until the internal temperature reaches 75°C and the breading is golden brown, flipping halfway through. Dollop each chicken breast with ¼ of the pesto and top with the Mozzarella. Return the breasts to the air fryer and cook for 3 minutes, or until the cheese is melted. Garnish with basil and serve with halved grape tomatoes on the side, if desired. Store leftovers in an airtight container in the refrigerator for up to 4 days. Reheat in a preheated 200°C air fryer for 5 minutes, or until warmed through.

Jerk Chicken Thighs

Prep time: 30 minutes | Cook time: 15 to 20 minutes | Serves 6

2 teaspoons ground coriander	½ teaspoon ground cinnamon
1 teaspoon ground allspice	½ teaspoon ground nutmeg
1 teaspoon cayenne pepper	900 g boneless chicken thighs,
1 teaspoon ground ginger	skin on
1 teaspoon salt	2 tablespoons olive oil
1 teaspoon dried thyme	

In a small bowl, combine the coriander, allspice, cayenne, ginger, salt, thyme, cinnamon, and nutmeg. Stir until thoroughly combined. Place the chicken in a baking dish and use paper towels to pat dry. Thoroughly coat both sides of the chicken with the spice mixture. Cover and refrigerate for at least 2 hours, preferably overnight. Preheat the air fryer to 180°C. Working in batches if necessary, arrange the chicken in a single layer in the air fryer basket and lightly coat with the olive oil. Pausing halfway through the cooking time to flip the chicken, air fry for 15 to 20 minutes, until a thermometer inserted into the thickest part registers 75°C.

Chicken and Broccoli Casserole

Prep time: 5 minutes | Cook time: 20 to 25 minutes | Serves 4

230 g broccoli, chopped into florets	½ teaspoon garlic powder
280 g shredded cooked chicken	Salt and freshly ground black pepper, to taste
115 g cream cheese	2 tablespoons chopped fresh
80 g heavy cream	basil
1½ teaspoons Dijon mustard	230 g shredded Cheddar cheese

Preheat the air fryer to 200°C. Lightly coat a casserole dish that will fit in air fryer, with olive oil and set aside. Place the broccoli in a large glass bowl with 1 tablespoon of water and cover with a microwavable plate. Microwave on high for 2 to 3 minutes until the broccoli is bright green but not mushy. Drain if necessary and add to another large bowl along with the shredded chicken. In the same glass bowl used to microwave the broccoli, combine the cream cheese and cream. Microwave for 30 seconds to 1 minute on high and stir until smooth. Add the mustard and garlic powder and season to taste with salt and freshly ground black pepper. Whisk until the sauce is smooth. Pour the warm sauce over the broccoli and chicken mixture and then add the basil. Using a silicone spatula, gently fold the mixture until thoroughly combined. Transfer the chicken mixture to the prepared casserole dish and top with the cheese. Air fry for 20 to 25 minutes until warmed through and the cheese has browned.

Garlic Parmesan Drumsticks

Prep time: 5 minutes | Cook time: 25 minutes | Serves 4

8 (115 g) chicken drumsticks
½ teaspoon salt
⅛ teaspoon ground black pepper

½ teaspoon garlic powder
2 tablespoons salted butter, melted
45 g grated Parmesan cheese
1 tablespoon dried parsley

Sprinkle drumsticks with salt, pepper, and garlic powder. Place drumsticks into ungreased air fryer basket. Adjust the temperature to 200°C and air fry for 25 minutes, turning drumsticks halfway through cooking. Drumsticks will be golden and have an internal temperature of at least 75°C when done. Transfer drumsticks to a large serving dish. Pour butter over drumsticks, and sprinkle with Parmesan and parsley. Serve warm.

Chicken Patties

Prep time: 15 minutes | Cook time: 12 minutes | Serves 4

450 g chicken thigh mince
110 g shredded Mozzarella cheese
1 teaspoon dried parsley

½ teaspoon garlic powder
¼ teaspoon onion powder
1 large egg
60 g pork rinds, finely ground

In a large bowl, mix chicken mince, Mozzarella, parsley, garlic powder, and onion powder. Form into four patties. Place patties in the freezer for 15 to 20 minutes until they begin to firm up. Whisk egg in a medium bowl. Place the ground pork rinds into a large bowl. Dip each chicken patty into the egg and then press into pork rinds to fully coat. Place patties into the air fryer basket. Adjust the temperature to 180°C and air fry for 12 minutes. Patties will be firm and cooked to an internal temperature of 75°C when done. Serve immediately.

Apricot-Glazed Chicken Drumsticks

Prep time: 15 minutes | Cook time: 30 minutes | Makes 6 drumsticks

For the Glaze:
160 g apricot preserves
½ teaspoon tamari
¼ teaspoon chili powder
2 teaspoons Dijon mustard
For the Chicken:

6 chicken drumsticks
½ teaspoon seasoning salt
1 teaspoon salt
½ teaspoon ground black pepper
Cooking spray

Make the glaze: Combine the ingredients for the glaze in a saucepan, then heat over low heat for 10 minutes or until thickened. Turn off the heat and sit until ready to use. Make the Chicken: Preheat the air fryer to 190°C. Spritz the air fryer basket with cooking spray. Combine the seasoning salt, salt, and pepper in a small bowl. Stir to mix well. Place the chicken drumsticks in the preheated air fryer. Spritz with cooking spray and sprinkle with the salt mixture on both sides. Air fry for 20 minutes or until well browned. Flip the chicken halfway through. Baste the chicken with the glaze and air fryer for 2 more minutes or until the chicken tenderloin is glossy. Serve immediately.

Pork Rind Fried Chicken

Prep time: 30 minutes | Cook time: 20 minutes | Serves 4

60 ml buffalo sauce
4 (115 g) boneless, skinless chicken breasts
½ teaspoon paprika
½ teaspoon garlic powder

¼ teaspoon ground black pepper
60 g g plain pork rinds, finely crushed

Pour buffalo sauce into a large sealable bowl or bag. Add chicken and toss to coat. Place sealed bowl or bag into refrigerator and let marinate at least 30 minutes up to overnight. Remove chicken from marinade but do not shake excess sauce off chicken. Sprinkle both sides of thighs with paprika, garlic powder, and pepper. Place pork rinds into a large bowl and press each chicken breast into pork rinds to coat evenly on both sides. Place chicken into ungreased air fryer basket. Adjust the temperature to 200°C and roast for 20 minutes, turning chicken halfway through cooking. Chicken will be golden and have an internal temperature of at least 75°C when done. Serve warm.

Chicken, Courgette, and Spinach Salad

Prep time: 10 minutes | Cook time: 20 minutes | Serves 4

3 (140 g) boneless, skinless chicken breasts, cut into 1-inch cubes
5 teaspoons extra-virgin olive oil
½ teaspoon dried thyme

1 medium red onion, sliced
1 red bell pepper, sliced
1 small courgette, cut into strips
3 tablespoons freshly squeezed lemon juice
85 g fresh baby spinach leaves

Insert the crisper plate into the basket and the basket into the unit. Preheat the unit by selecting AIR ROAST, setting the temperature to 190°C, and setting the time to 3 minutes. Select START/STOP to begin. In a large bowl, combine the chicken, olive oil, and thyme. Toss to coat. Transfer to a medium metal bowl that fits into the basket. Once the unit is preheated, place the bowl into the basket. Select AIR ROAST, set the temperature to 190°C, and set the time to 20 minutes. Select START/STOP to begin. After 8 minutes, add the red onion, red bell pepper, and courgette to the bowl. Resume cooking. After about 6 minutes more, stir the chicken and vegetables. Resume cooking. When the cooking is complete, a food thermometer inserted into the chicken should register at least 75°C. Remove the bowl from the unit and stir in the lemon juice. Put the spinach in a serving bowl and top with the chicken mixture. Toss to combine and serve immediately.

Chicken Schnitzel

Prep time: 15 minutes | Cook time: 5 minutes | Serves 4

60 g all-purpose flour
1 teaspoon marjoram
½ teaspoon thyme
1 teaspoon dried parsley flakes
½ teaspoon salt
1 egg

1 teaspoon lemon juice
1 teaspoon water
120 g breadcrumbs
4 chicken tenders, pounded
thin, cut in half lengthwise
Cooking spray

Preheat the air fryer to 200ºC and spritz with cooking spray. Combine the flour, marjoram, thyme, parsley, and salt in a shallow dish. Stir to mix well. Whisk the egg with lemon juice and water in a large bowl. Pour the breadcrumbs in a separate shallow dish. Roll the chicken halves in the flour mixture first, then in the egg mixture, and then roll over the breadcrumbs to coat well. Shake the excess off. Arrange the chicken halves in the preheated air fryer and spritz with cooking spray on both sides. Air fry for 5 minutes or until the chicken halves are golden brown and crispy. Flip the halves halfway through. Serve immediately.

Celery Chicken

Prep time: 10 minutes | Cook time: 15 minutes |

Serves 4

120 ml soy sauce
2 tablespoons hoisin sauce
4 teaspoons minced garlic
1 teaspoon freshly ground black
pepper

8 boneless, skinless chicken
tenderloins
120 g chopped celery
1 medium red bell pepper, diced
Olive oil spray

Preheat the air fryer to 190ºC. Spray the air fryer basket lightly with olive oil spray. In a large bowl, mix together the soy sauce, hoisin sauce, garlic, and black pepper to make a marinade. Add the chicken, celery, and bell pepper and toss to coat. Shake the excess marinade off the chicken, place it and the vegetables in the air fryer basket, and lightly spray with olive oil spray. You may need to cook them in batches. Reserve the remaining marinade. Air fry for 8 minutes. Turn the chicken over and brush with some of the remaining marinade. Air fry for an additional 5 to 7 minutes, or until the chicken reaches an internal temperature of at least 75ºC. Serve.

Spanish Chicken and Mini Sweet Pepper Baguette

Prep time: 10 minutes | Cook time: 20 minutes | Serves 2

570 g assorted small chicken
parts, breasts cut into halves
¼ teaspoon salt
¼ teaspoon ground black
pepper
2 teaspoons olive oil

230 g mini sweet peppers
60 g light mayonnaise
¼ teaspoon smoked paprika
½ clove garlic, crushed
Baguette, for serving
Cooking spray

Preheat air fryer to 190ºC. Spritz the air fryer basket with cooking spray. Toss the chicken with salt, ground black pepper, and olive oil in a large bowl. Arrange the sweet peppers and chicken in the preheated air fryer and air fry for 10 minutes, then transfer the peppers on a plate. Flip the chicken and air fry for 10 more minutes or until well browned. Meanwhile, combine the mayo, paprika, and garlic in a small bowl. Stir to mix well. Assemble the baguette with chicken and sweet pepper, then spread with mayo mixture and serve.

Turkish Chicken Kebabs

Prep time: 30 minutes | Cook time: 15 minutes | Serves 4

70 g plain Greek yogurt
1 tablespoon minced garlic
1 tablespoon tomato paste
1 tablespoon fresh lemon juice
1 tablespoon vegetable oil
1 teaspoon kosher salt
1 teaspoon ground cumin

1 teaspoon sweet Hungarian
paprika
½ teaspoon ground cinnamon
½ teaspoon black pepper
½ teaspoon cayenne pepper
450 g boneless, skinless chicken
thighs, quartered crosswise

In a large bowl, combine the yogurt, garlic, tomato paste, lemon juice, vegetable oil, salt, cumin, paprika, cinnamon, black pepper, and cayenne. Stir until the spices are blended into the yogurt. Add the chicken to the bowl and toss until well coated. Marinate at room temperature for 30 minutes, or cover and refrigerate for up to 24 hours. Arrange the chicken in a single layer in the air fryer basket. Set the air fryer to (190ºC for 10 minutes. Turn the chicken and cook for 5 minutes more. Use a meat thermometer to ensure the chicken has reached an internal temperature of 75ºC.

Barbecued Chicken with Creamy Coleslaw

Prep time: 10 minutes | Cook time: 20 minutes | Serves 2

270 g shredded coleslaw mix
Salt and pepper
2 (340 g) bone-in split chicken
breasts, trimmed
1 teaspoon vegetable oil
2 tablespoons barbecue sauce,

plus extra for serving
2 tablespoons mayonnaise
2 tablespoons sour cream
1 teaspoon distilled white
vinegar, plus extra for seasoning
¼ teaspoon sugar

Preheat the air fryer to 180ºC. Toss coleslaw mix and ¼ teaspoon salt in a colander set over bowl. Let sit until wilted slightly, about 30 minutes. Rinse, drain, and dry well with a dish towel. Meanwhile, pat chicken dry with paper towels, rub with oil, and season with salt and pepper. Arrange breasts skin-side down in air fryer basket, spaced evenly apart, alternating ends. Bake for 10 minutes. Flip breasts and brush skin side with barbecue sauce. Return basket to air fryer and bake until well browned and chicken registers 70ºC, 10 to 15 minutes. Transfer chicken to serving platter, tent loosely with aluminum foil, and let rest for 5 minutes. While chicken rests, whisk mayonnaise, sour cream, vinegar, sugar, and pinch pepper together in a large bowl. Stir in coleslaw mix and season with salt, pepper, and additional vinegar to taste. Serve chicken with coleslaw, passing extra barbecue sauce separately.

Chapter 7 Desserts

Biscuit-Base Cheesecake

Prep time: 10 minutes | Cook time: 20 minutes | Serves 8

100 g crushed digestive biscuits	65 g granulated sugar
3 tablespoons butter, at room temperature	2 eggs, beaten
	1 tablespoon all-purpose flour
225 g cream cheese, at room temperature	1 teaspoon vanilla extract
	60 ml chocolate syrup

In a small bowl, stir together the crushed biscuits and butter. Press the crust into the bottom of a 6-by-2-inch round baking pan and freeze to set while you prepare the filling. In a medium bowl, stir together the cream cheese and sugar until mixed well. One at a time, beat in the eggs. Add the flour and vanilla and stir to combine. Transfer ⅓ of the filling to a small bowl and stir in the chocolate syrup until combined. Insert the crisper plate into the basket and the basket into the unit. Preheat the air fryer to 165°C, and bake for 3 minutes. Pour the vanilla filling into the pan with the crust. Drop the chocolate filling over the vanilla filling by the spoonful. With a clean butter knife stir the fillings in a zigzag pattern to marble them. Do not let the knife touch the crust. Once the unit is preheated, place the pan into the basket. Set the temperature to 165°C, and bake for 20 minutes. When the cooking is done, the cheesecake should be just set. Cool on a wire rack for 1 hour. Refrigerate the cheesecake until firm before slicing.

Strawberry Pastry Rolls

Prep time: 20 minutes | Cook time: 5 to 6 minutes per batch | Serves 4

85 g low-fat cream cheese	8 sheets filo pastry
2 tablespoons plain yogurt	Butter-flavored cooking spray
2 teaspoons granulated sugar	45-90 g dark chocolate chips
¼ teaspoon pure vanilla extract	(optional)
225 g fresh strawberries	

In a medium bowl, combine the cream cheese, yogurt, sugar, and vanilla. Beat with hand mixer at high speed until smooth (about 1 minute). Wash strawberries and destem. Chop enough of them to measure 80 g. Stir into cheese mixture. Preheat the air fryer to 165°C. Filo pastry dries out quickly, so cover your stack of filo sheets with baking paper and then place a damp dish towel on top of that. Remove only one sheet at a time as you work. To create one pastry roll, lay out a single sheet of filo. Spray lightly with butter-flavored spray, top with a second sheet of filo and spray the second sheet lightly. Place a quarter of the filling (about 3 tablespoons) about ½ inch from the edge of one short side. Fold the end of the pastry over the filling and keep rolling a turn or two. Fold in both the left and right sides so that the edges meet in the middle of your roll. Then roll up completely. Spray outside of pastry roll with butter spray. When you have 4 rolls, place them in the air fryer basket, seam side down, leaving some space in between each. Air fry for 5 to 6 minutes, until they turn a delicate golden brown. Repeat step 7 for remaining rolls. Allow pastries to cool to room temperature. 1When ready to serve, slice the remaining strawberries. If desired, melt the chocolate chips in microwave or double boiler. Place 1 pastry on each dessert plate, and top with sliced strawberries. Drizzle melted chocolate over strawberries and onto plate.

Crumbly Coconut-Pecan Cookies

Prep time: 10 minutes | Cook time: 25 minutes | Serves 10

170 g coconut flour	150 g monk fruit, or equivalent
170 g extra-fine almond flour	sweetener
½ teaspoon baking powder	¼ teaspoon freshly grated
⅓ teaspoon baking soda	nutmeg
3 eggs plus an egg yolk, beaten	⅓ teaspoon ground cloves
175 ml coconut oil, at room	½ teaspoon pure vanilla extract
temperature	½ teaspoon pure coconut
125 g unsalted pecan nuts,	extract
roughly chopped	⅛ teaspoon fine sea salt

Preheat the air fryer to 190°C. Line the air fryer basket with baking paper. Mix the coconut flour, almond flour, baking powder, and baking soda in a large mixing bowl. In another mixing bowl, stir together the eggs and coconut oil. Add the wet mixture to the dry mixture. Mix in the remaining ingredients and stir until a soft dough forms. Drop about 2 tablespoons of dough on the baking paper for each cookie and flatten each biscuit until it's 1 inch thick. Bake for about 25 minutes until the cookies are golden and firm to the touch. Remove from the basket to a plate. Let the cookies cool to room temperature and serve.

Oatmeal Raisin Bars

Prep time: 15 minutes | Cook time: 15 minutes | Serves 8

40 g plain flour	50 g granulated sugar
¼ teaspoon kosher, or coarse sea salt	120 ml canola, or rapeseed oil
¼ teaspoon baking powder	1 large egg
¼ teaspoon ground cinnamon	1 teaspoon vanilla extract
50 g light brown sugar, lightly packed	110 g quick-cooking oats
	60 g raisins

Preheat the air fryer to 185°C. In a large bowl, combine the plain flour, kosher salt, baking powder, ground cinnamon, light brown sugar, granulated sugar, canola oil, egg, vanilla extract, quick-cooking oats, and raisins. Spray a baking pan with nonstick cooking spray, then pour the oat mixture into the pan and press down to evenly distribute. Place the pan in the air fryer and bake for 15 minutes or until golden brown. Remove from the air fryer and allow to cool in the pan on a wire rack for 20 minutes before slicing and serving.

Chocolate Chip Pecan Biscotti

Prep time: 15 minutes | Cook time: 20 to 22 minutes | Serves 10

135 g finely ground blanched almond flour	1 large egg, beaten
¾ teaspoon baking powder	1 teaspoon pure vanilla extract
½ teaspoon xanthan gum	50 g chopped pecans
¼ teaspoon sea salt	40 g organic chocolate chips,
3 tablespoons unsalted butter, at room temperature	Melted organic chocolate chips and chopped pecans, for topping (optional)
35 g powdered sweetener	

In a large bowl, combine the almond flour, baking powder, xanthan gum, and salt. Line a cake pan that fits inside your air fryer with baking paper. In the bowl of a stand mixer, beat together the butter and powdered sweetener. Add the beaten egg and vanilla and beat for about 3 minutes. Add the almond flour mixture to the butter and egg mixture; beat until just combined. Stir in the pecans and chocolate chips. Transfer the dough to the prepared pan and press it into the bottom. Set the air fryer to 165°C and bake for 12 minutes. Remove from the air fryer and let cool for 15 minutes. Using a sharp knife, cut the cookie into thin strips, then return the strips to the cake pan with the bottom sides facing up. Set the air fryer to 150°C. Bake for 8 to 10 minutes. Remove from the air fryer and let cool completely on a wire rack. If desired, dip one side of each biscotti piece into melted chocolate chips, and top with chopped pecans.

New York Cheesecake

Prep time: 1 hour | Cook time: 37 minutes | Serves 8

170 g almond flour	340 g granulated sweetener
85 g powdered sweetener	3 eggs, at room temperature
55 g unsalted butter, melted	1 tablespoon vanilla essence
565 g full-fat cream cheese	1 teaspoon grated lemon zest
120 ml heavy cream	

Coat the sides and bottom of a baking pan with a little flour. In a mixing bowl, combine the almond flour and powdered sweetener. Add the melted butter and mix until your mixture looks like breadcrumbs. Press the mixture into the bottom of the prepared pan to form an even layer. Bake at 165°C for 7 minutes until golden brown. Allow it to cool completely on a wire rack. Meanwhile, in a mixer fitted with the paddle attachment, prepare the filling by mixing the soft cheese, heavy cream, and granulated sweetener; beat until creamy and fluffy. Crack the eggs into the mixing bowl, one at a time; add the vanilla and lemon zest and continue to mix until fully combined. Pour the prepared topping over the cooled crust and spread evenly. Bake in the preheated air fryer at 165°C for 25 to 30 minutes; leave it in the air fryer to keep warm for another 30 minutes. Cover your cheesecake with plastic wrap. Place in your refrigerator and allow it to cool at least 6 hours or overnight. Serve well chilled.

Fried Cheesecake Bites

Prep time: 30 minutes | Cook time: 2 minutes | Makes 16 bites

225 g cream cheese, softened	divided
50 g powdered sweetener, plus 2 tablespoons, divided	½ teaspoon vanilla extract
4 tablespoons heavy cream,	50 g almond flour

In a stand mixer fitted with a paddle attachment, beat the cream cheese, 50 g of the sweetener, 2 tablespoons of the heavy cream, and the vanilla until smooth. Using a small ice-cream scoop, divide the mixture into 16 balls and arrange them on a rimmed baking sheet lined with baking paper. Freeze for 45 minutes until firm. Line the air fryer basket with baking paper and preheat the air fryer to 175°C. In a small shallow bowl, combine the almond flour with the remaining 2 tablespoons of sweetener. In another small shallow bowl, place the remaining 2 tablespoons cream. One at a time, dip the frozen cheesecake balls into the cream and then roll in the almond flour mixture, pressing lightly to form an even coating. Arrange the balls in a single layer in the air fryer basket, leaving room between them. Air fry for 2 minutes until the coating is lightly browned.

Baked Brazilian Pineapple

Prep time: 10 minutes | Cook time: 10 minutes | Serves 4

95 g brown sugar

2 teaspoons ground cinnamon

1 small pineapple, peeled,

cored, and cut into spears

3 tablespoons unsalted butter, melted

In a small bowl, mix the brown sugar and cinnamon until thoroughly combined. Brush the pineapple spears with the melted butter. Sprinkle the cinnamon-sugar over the spears, pressing lightly to ensure it adheres well. Place the spears in the air fryer basket in a single layer. (Depending on the size of your air fryer, you may have to do this in batches.) Set the air fryer to 200ºC and cook for 10 minutes for the first batch (6 to 8 minutes for the next batch, as the fryer will be preheated). Halfway through the cooking time, brush the spears with butter. The pineapple spears are done when they are heated through, and the sugar is bubbling. Serve hot.

Pumpkin Spice Pecans

Prep time: 5 minutes | Cook time: 6 minutes | Serves 4

125 g whole pecans

50 g granulated sweetener

1 large egg white

½ teaspoon ground cinnamon

½ teaspoon pumpkin pie spice

½ teaspoon vanilla extract

Toss all ingredients in a large bowl until pecans are coated. Place into the air fryer basket. Adjust the temperature to 150ºC and air fry for 6 minutes. Toss two to three times during cooking. Allow to cool completely. Store in an airtight container up to 3 days.

5-Ingredient Brownies

Prep time: 10 minutes | Cook time: 25 minutes | Serves 6

Vegetable oil

110 g unsalted butter

½ cup chocolate chips

3 large eggs

100 g granulated sugar

1 teaspoon pure vanilla extract

Generously grease a baking pan with vegetable oil. In a microwave-safe bowl, combine the butter and chocolate chips. Microwave on high for 1 minute. Stir very well. (You want the heat from the butter and chocolate to melt the remaining clumps. If you microwave until everything melts, the chocolate will be overcooked. If necessary, microwave for an additional 10 seconds, but stir well before you try that.) In a medium bowl, combine the eggs, sugar, and vanilla. Whisk until light and frothy. Whisking continuously, slowly pour in the melted chocolate in a thin stream and whisk until everything is incorporated. Pour the batter into the prepared pan. Set the pan in the air fryer basket. Set the air fryer to 175ºC, and bake for 25 minutes, or until a toothpick inserted into the center comes out clean. Let cool in the pan on a wire rack for 30 minutes before cutting into squares.

Cinnamon and Pecan Pie

Prep time: 10 minutes | Cook time: 25 minutes | Serves 4

1 pack shortcrust pastry

½ teaspoons cinnamon

¾ teaspoon vanilla extract

2 eggs

175 ml maple syrup

⅛ teaspoon nutmeg

3 tablespoons melted butter, divided

2 tablespoons sugar

65 g chopped pecans

Preheat the air fryer to 190ºC. In a small bowl, coat the pecans in 1 tablespoon of melted butter. Transfer the pecans to the air fryer and air fry for about 10 minutes. Put the pie dough in a greased pie pan, trim off the excess and add the pecans on top. In a bowl, mix the rest of the ingredients. Pour this over the pecans. Put the pan in the air fryer and bake for 25 minutes. Serve immediately.

Molten Chocolate Almond Cakes

Prep time: 5 minutes | Cook time: 13 minutes | Serves 3

Butter and flour for the ramekins

110 g bittersweet chocolate, chopped

110 g unsalted butter

2 eggs

2 egg yolks

50 g granulated sugar

½ teaspoon pure vanilla extract,

or almond extract

1 tablespoon plain flour

3 tablespoons ground almonds

8 to 12 semisweet chocolate discs (or 4 chunks of chocolate)

Cocoa powder or icing sugar, for dusting

Toasted almonds, coarsely chopped

Butter and flour three (170 g) ramekins. (Butter the ramekins and then coat the butter with flour by shaking it around in the ramekin and dumping out any excess.) Melt the chocolate and butter together, either in the microwave or in a double boiler. In a separate bowl, beat the eggs, egg yolks and sugar together until light and smooth. Add the vanilla extract. Whisk the chocolate mixture into the egg mixture. Stir in the flour and ground almonds. Preheat the air fryer to 165ºC. Transfer the batter carefully to the buttered ramekins, filling halfway. Place two or three chocolate discs in the center of the batter and then fill the ramekins to ½-inch below the top with the remaining batter. Place the ramekins into the air fryer basket and air fry for 13 minutes. The sides of the cake should be set, but the centers should be slightly soft. Remove the ramekins from the air fryer and let the cakes sit for 5 minutes. (If you'd like the cake a little less molten, air fry for 14 minutes and let the cakes sit for 4 minutes.) Run a butter knife around the edge of the ramekins and invert the cakes onto a plate. Lift the ramekin off the plate slowly and carefully so that the cake doesn't break. Dust with cocoa powder or icing sugar and serve with a scoop of ice cream and some coarsely chopped toasted almonds.

Cardamom Custard

Prep time: 10 minutes | Cook time: 25 minutes | Serves 2

240 ml whole milk

1 large egg

2 tablespoons granulated sugar, plus 1 teaspoon

¼ teaspoon vanilla bean paste or pure vanilla extract

¼ teaspoon ground cardamom, plus more for sprinkling

In a medium bowl, beat together the milk, egg, sugar, vanilla, and cardamom. Place two ramekins in the air fryer basket. Divide the mixture between the ramekins. Sprinkle lightly with cardamom. Cover each ramekin tightly with aluminum foil. Set the air fryer to 175°C and cook for 25 minutes, or until a toothpick inserted in the center comes out clean. Let the custards cool on a wire rack for 5 to 10 minutes. Serve warm or refrigerate until cold and serve chilled.

Butter Flax Cookies

Prep time: 25 minutes | Cook time: 20 minutes | Serves 4

225 g almond meal

2 tablespoons flaxseed meal

30 g monk fruit, or equivalent sweetener

1 teaspoon baking powder

A pinch of grated nutmeg

A pinch of coarse salt

1 large egg, room temperature.

110 g unsalted butter, room temperature

1 teaspoon vanilla extract

Mix the almond meal, flaxseed meal, monk fruit, baking powder, grated nutmeg, and salt in a bowl. In a separate bowl, whisk the egg, butter, and vanilla extract. Stir the egg mixture into dry mixture; mix to combine well or until it forms a nice, soft dough. Roll your dough out and cut out with a cookie cutter of your choice. Bake in the preheated air fryer at 175°C for 10 minutes. Decrease the temperature to 165°C and cook for 10 minutes longer. Bon appétit!

Hazelnut Butter Cookies

Prep time: 30 minutes | Cook time: 20 minutes | Serves 10

4 tablespoons liquid monk fruit, or agave syrup

65 g hazelnuts, ground

110 g unsalted butter, room temperature

190 g almond flour

110 g coconut flour

55 g granulated sweetener

2 teaspoons ground cinnamon

Firstly, cream liquid monk fruit with butter until the mixture becomes fluffy. Sift in both types of flour. Now, stir in the hazelnuts. Now, knead the mixture to form a dough; place in the refrigerator for about 35 minutes. To finish, shape the prepared dough into the bite-sized balls; arrange them on a baking dish; flatten the balls

using the back of a spoon. Mix granulated sweetener with ground cinnamon. Press your cookies in the cinnamon mixture until they are completely covered. Bake the cookies for 20 minutes at 155°C. Leave them to cool for about 10 minutes before transferring them to a wire rack. Bon appétit!

Almond Butter Cookie Balls

Prep time: 5 minutes | Cook time: 10 minutes | Makes 10 balls

70 g almond butter

1 large egg

1 teaspoon vanilla extract

30 g low-carb protein powder

30 g powdered sweetener

25 g desiccated unsweetened coconut

40 g low-carb, sugar-free chocolate chips

½ teaspoon ground cinnamon

In a large bowl, mix almond butter and egg. Add in vanilla, protein powder, and sweetener. Fold in coconut, chocolate chips, and cinnamon. Roll into 1-inch balls. Place balls into a round baking pan and put into the air fryer basket. Adjust the temperature to 160°C and bake for 10 minutes. Allow to cool completely. Store in an airtight container in the refrigerator up to 4 days.

Luscious Coconut Pie

Prep time: 5 minutes | Cook time: 45 minutes | Serves 6

100 g desiccated, unsweetened coconut, plus 25 g, divided

2 eggs

355 ml almond milk

100 g granulated sweetener

55 g coconut flour

55 g unsalted butter, melted

1½ teaspoons vanilla extract

¼ teaspoon salt

2 tablespoons powdered sweetener (optional)

120 g whipping cream, whipped until stiff (optional)

Spread 25 g of the coconut in the bottom of a pie plate and place in the air fryer basket. Set the air fryer to 175°C and air fry the coconut while the air fryer preheats, about 5 minutes, until golden brown. Transfer the coconut to a small bowl and set aside for garnish. Brush the pie plate with oil and set aside. In a large bowl, combine the remaining 100 g shredded coconut, eggs, milk, granulated sweetener, coconut flour, butter, vanilla, and salt. Whisk until smooth. Pour the batter into the prepared pie plate and air fry for 40 to 45 minutes, or until a toothpick inserted into the center of the pie comes out clean. (Check halfway through the baking time and rotate the pan, if necessary, for even baking.) Remove the pie from the air fryer and place on a baking rack to cool completely. Garnish with the reserved toasted coconut and the powdered sweetener or whipped cream, if desired. Cover and refrigerate leftover pie for up to 3 days.

Tortilla Fried Hand Pies

Prep time: 10 minutes | Cook time: 5 minutes per batch | Makes 12 pies

12 small flour tortillas (4-inch diameter)	2 tablespoons desiccated, unsweetened coconut
160 g fig jam	Coconut, or avocado oil for misting or cooking spray
20 g slivered almonds	

Wrap refrigerated tortillas in damp paper towels and heat in microwave 30 seconds to warm. Working with one tortilla at a time, place 2 teaspoons fig jam, 1 teaspoon slivered almonds, and ½ teaspoon coconut in the center of each. Moisten outer edges of tortilla all around. Fold one side of tortilla over filling, to make a half-moon shape, and press down lightly on center. Using the tines of a fork, press down firmly on edges of tortilla to seal in filling. Mist both sides with oil or cooking spray. Place hand pies in air fryer basket, close, but not overlapping. It's fine to lean some against the sides and corners of the basket. You may need to cook in 2 batches. Air fry at 200°C for 5 minutes, or until lightly browned. Serve hot. Refrigerate any leftover pies in a closed container. To serve later, toss them back in the air fryer basket and cook for 2 to 3 minutes to reheat.

Chocolate Chip Cookie Cake

Prep time: 5 minutes | Cook time: 15 minutes | Serves 8

4 tablespoons salted butter, melted	110 g blanched finely ground almond flour
65 g granular brown sweetener	½ teaspoon baking powder
1 large egg	40 g low-carb chocolate chips
½ teaspoon vanilla extract	

In a large bowl, whisk together butter, sweetener, egg, and vanilla. Add flour and baking powder and stir until combined. Fold in chocolate chips, then spoon batter into an ungreased round nonstick baking dish. Place dish into air fryer basket. Adjust the temperature to 150°C and set the timer for 15 minutes. When edges are browned, cookie cake will be done. Slice and serve warm.

Roasted Honey Pears

Prep time: 7 minutes | Cook time: 18 to 23 minutes | Serves 4

2 large Bosc pears, halved lengthwise and seeded	½ teaspoon ground cinnamon
3 tablespoons honey	30 g walnuts, chopped
1 tablespoon unsalted butter	55 g part-skim ricotta cheese, divided

Insert the crisper plate into the basket and the basket into the unit.

Preheat to 175°C. In a 6-by-2-inch round pan, place the pears cut-side up. In a small microwave-safe bowl, melt the honey, butter, and cinnamon. Brush this mixture over the cut sides of the pears. Pour 3 tablespoons of water around the pears in the pan. Once the unit is preheated, place the pan into the basket. After about 18 minutes, check the pears. They should be tender when pierced with a fork and slightly crisp on the edges. If not, resume cooking. When the cooking is complete, baste the pears once with the liquid in the pan. Carefully remove the pears from the pan and place on a serving plate. Drizzle each with some liquid from the pan, sprinkle the walnuts on top, and serve with a spoonful of ricotta cheese.

Apple Fries

Prep time: 10 minutes | Cook time: 7 minutes | Serves 8

Coconut, or avocado oil, for spraying	55 g granulated sugar
110 g plain flour	1 teaspoon ground cinnamon
3 large eggs, beaten	3 large Gala apples, peeled, cored and cut into wedges
100 g crushed digestive biscuits	240 ml caramel sauce, warmed

Preheat the air fryer to 190°C. Line the air fryer basket with baking paper and spray lightly with oil. Place the flour and beaten eggs in separate bowls and set aside. In another bowl, mix together the crushed biscuits, sugar and cinnamon. Working one at a time, coat the apple wedges in the flour, dip in the egg and then dredge in the biscuit mix until evenly coated. Place the apples in the prepared basket, taking care not to overlap, and spray lightly with oil. You may need to work in batches, depending on the size of your air fryer. Cook for 5 minutes, flip, spray with oil, and cook for another 2 minutes, or until crunchy and golden brown. Drizzle the caramel sauce over the top and serve.

Protein Powder Doughnut Holes

Prep time: 25 minutes | Cook time: 6 minutes | Makes 12 holes

50 g blanched finely ground almond flour	½ teaspoon baking powder
60 g low-carb vanilla protein powder	1 large egg
	5 tablespoons unsalted butter, melted
100 g granulated sweetener	½ teaspoon vanilla extract

Mix all ingredients in a large bowl. Place into the freezer for 20 minutes. Wet your hands with water and roll the dough into twelve balls. Cut a piece of baking paper to fit your air fryer basket. Working in batches as necessary, place doughnut holes into the air fryer basket on top of baking paper. Adjust the temperature to 190°C and air fry for 6 minutes. Flip doughnut holes halfway through the cooking time. Let cool completely before serving.

Coconut-Custard Pie

Prep time: 10 minutes | Cook time: 20 to 23 minutes | Serves 4

240 ml milk	2 eggs
50 g granulated sugar, plus 2 tablespoons	2 tablespoons melted butter
30 g scone mix	Cooking spray
1 teaspoon vanilla extract	50 g desiccated, sweetened coconut

Place all ingredients except coconut in a medium bowl. Using a hand mixer, beat on high speed for 3 minutes. Let sit for 5 minutes. Preheat the air fryer to 165°C. Spray a baking pan with cooking spray and place pan in air fryer basket. Pour filling into pan and sprinkle coconut over top. Cook pie for 20 to 23 minutes or until center sets.

Apple Wedges with Apricots

Prep time: 5 minutes | Cook time: 15 to 18 minutes | Serves 4

4 large apples, peeled and sliced into 8 wedges	1 to 2 tablespoons granulated sugar
2 tablespoons light olive oil	½ teaspoon ground cinnamon
95 g dried apricots, chopped	

Preheat the air fryer to 180°C. Toss the apple wedges with the olive oil in a mixing bowl until well coated. Place the apple wedges in the air fryer basket and air fry for 12 to 15 minutes. Sprinkle with the dried apricots and air fry for another 3 minutes. Meanwhile, thoroughly combine the sugar and cinnamon in a small bowl. Remove the apple wedges from the basket to a plate. Serve sprinkled with the sugar mixture.

Chickpea Brownies

Prep time: 10 minutes | Cook time: 20 minutes | Serves 6

Vegetable oil	cocoa powder
425 g can chickpeas, drained and rinsed	1 tablespoon espresso powder (optional)
4 large eggs	1 teaspoon baking powder
80 ml coconut oil, melted	1 teaspoon baking soda
80 ml honey	80 g chocolate chips
3 tablespoons unsweetened	

Preheat the air fryer to 165°C. Generously grease a baking pan with vegetable oil. In a blender or food processor, combine the chickpeas, eggs, coconut oil, honey, cocoa powder, espresso powder (if using), baking powder, and baking soda. Blend or process until smooth. Transfer to the prepared pan and stir in the chocolate chips

by hand. Set the pan in the air fryer basket and bake for 20 minutes, or until a toothpick inserted into the center comes out clean. Let cool in the pan on a wire rack for 30 minutes before cutting into squares. Serve immediately.

Spiced Apple Cake

Prep time: 15 minutes | Cook time: 30 minutes | Serves 6

Vegetable oil	1 tablespoon apple pie spice
2 diced & peeled Gala apples	½ teaspoon ground ginger
1 tablespoon fresh lemon juice	¼ teaspoon ground cardamom
55 g unsalted butter, softened	¼ teaspoon ground nutmeg
65 g granulated sugar	½ teaspoon kosher, or coarse sea salt
2 large eggs	60 ml whole milk
155 g plain flour	Icing sugar, for dusting
1½ teaspoons baking powder	

Grease a 0.7-liter Bundt, or tube pan with oil; set aside. In a medium bowl, toss the apples with the lemon juice until well coated; set aside. In a large bowl, combine the butter and sugar. Beat with an electric hand mixer on medium speed until the sugar has dissolved. Add the eggs and beat until fluffy. Add the flour, baking powder, apple pie spice, ginger, cardamom, nutmeg, salt, and milk. Mix until the batter is thick but pourable. Pour the batter into the prepared pan. Top batter evenly with the apple mixture. Place the pan in the air fryer basket. Set the air fryer to 175°C and cook for 30 minutes, or until a toothpick inserted in the center of the cake comes out clean. Close the air fryer and let the cake rest for 10 minutes. Turn the cake out onto a wire rack and cool completely. Right before serving, dust the cake with icing sugar.

Grilled Peaches

Prep time: 5 minutes | Cook time: 10 minutes | Serves 4

Coconut, or avocado oil, for spraying	¼ teaspoon cinnamon
25 g crushed digestive biscuits	2 peaches, pitted and cut into quarters
50 g packed light brown sugar	4 scoops vanilla ice cream
8 tablespoons unsalted butter	

Line the air fryer basket with baking paper, and spray lightly with oil. In a small bowl, mix together the crushed biscuits, brown sugar, butter, and cinnamon with a fork until crumbly. Place the peach wedges in the prepared basket, skin-side up. You may need to work in batches, depending on the size of your air fryer. Air fry at 175°C for 5 minutes, flip, and sprinkle with a spoonful of the biscuit mixture. Cook for another 5 minutes, or until tender and caramelized. Top with a scoop of vanilla ice cream and any remaining crumble mixture. Serve immediately.

Indian Toast and Milk

Prep time: 10 minutes | Cook time: 20 minutes | Serves 4

305 g sweetened, condensed milk

240 ml evaporated milk

240 ml single cream

1 teaspoon ground cardamom, plus additional for garnish

1 pinch saffron threads

4 slices white bread

2 to 3 tablespoons ghee or butter, softened

2 tablespoons crushed pistachios, for garnish (optional)

In a baking pan, combine the condensed milk, evaporated milk, half-and-half, cardamom, and saffron. Stir until well combined. Place the pan in the air fryer basket. Set the air fryer to 175°C for 15 minutes, stirring halfway through the cooking time. Remove the sweetened milk from the air fryer and set aside. Cut each slice of bread into two triangles. Brush each side with ghee. Place the bread in the air fryer basket. Keeping the air fryer on 175°C cook for 5 minutes or until golden brown and toasty. Remove the bread from the air fryer. Arrange two triangles in each of four wide, shallow bowls. Pour the hot milk mixture on top of the bread and let soak for 30 minutes. Garnish with pistachios if using, and sprinkle with additional cardamom.

Vanilla Scones

Prep time: 20 minutes | Cook time: 10 minutes | Serves 6

110 g coconut flour

½ teaspoon baking powder

1 teaspoon apple cider vinegar

2 teaspoons mascarpone

60 ml heavy cream

1 teaspoon vanilla extract

1 tablespoon granulated sweetener

Cooking spray

In the mixing bowl, mix coconut flour with baking powder, apple cider vinegar, mascarpone, heavy cream, vanilla extract, and sweetener. Knead the dough and cut into scones. Then put them in the air fryer basket and sprinkle with cooking spray. Cook the vanilla scones at 185°C for 10 minutes.

Chocolate Cake

Prep time: 10 minutes | Cook time: 20 to 23 minutes | Serves 8

100 g granulated sugar

30 g plain flour, plus 3 tablespoons

3 tablespoons cocoa

½ teaspoon baking powder

½ teaspoon baking soda

¼ teaspoon salt

1 egg

2 tablespoons oil

120 ml milk

½ teaspoon vanilla extract

Preheat the air fryer to 165°C. Grease and flour a baking pan. In a medium bowl, stir together the sugar, flour, cocoa, baking powder, baking soda, and salt. Add all other ingredients and beat with a wire whisk until smooth. Pour batter into prepared pan and bake for 20 to 23 minutes, until toothpick inserted in center comes out clean, or with crumbs clinging to it.

Printed in Great Britain
by Amazon

22151396R00037